Richard H. Akeroyd

THE SPIRITUAL QUEST
OF
Albert Camus

A PORTALS BOOK

Portals Press, P.O. Box 1048
Tuscaloosa, Alabama 35401

ISBN 0-916620-03-4

Library of Congress Card Catalog Number 76-3324

Manufactured in the United States of America

This book was composed in Linotype Garamond and Janson and in foundry Caslon Old Style by William Foley Typesetting at Compton, California, and was printed and bound by George Banta Company, Inc. at Menasha, Wisconsin. Book design by Travis James.

Preface

It has been generally accepted that the main significance of Camus's work is spiritual. "The spiritual guide of many a confused and searching soul," Henri Peyre calls him. (BV, 65) Philosophers find a place for him, although he avowed he was not one of them himself. Novelists and playwrights acknowledge his extraordinary gift. Theologians are fascinated by his perception. Yet it is "everyman," and not just the specialist, who understands and can relate to the "quest, rather than a message" of which he wrote. (BH, II, 451)

His quest related to man. Though he believed that "the earth has no superior meaning," he nevertheless affirmed: "something in it makes sense and that is man, because he is the only being who insists upon it. This world has at least the truth of man." (CE, 241)

His work, which was twofold, would portray the nature and spiritual state of man and of the society he has created, and the principles which motivate him or bind him in his heart; and would seek out a satisfactory "raison d'être" for his existence, a sufficient answer to this "desire for unity, this longing for clarity and cohesion." (CM, 38) What he portrayed are the truths of man; what he sought out, had he found it, would have been man's truth.

This book is concerned with a spiritual quest. It examines and elucidates the truths Camus perceived, and follows his quest for *truth*, observing the point at which his quest was arrested.

R. H. A.

Acknowledgments

I express my gratitude to Mme Jacqueline Bernard for her permission to cite the anecdote in chapter five relating to her experiences when she worked with Camus on the underground resistance newspaper *Combat* in Paris during World War II.

Alfred A. Knopf Inc., the holder of the exclusive United States rights to all Camus's works in French and in translation, kindly granted permission for all the quotations from his works and for my own translations into English of certain passages.

Published translations from the French are used save when, to demonstrate a thesis, a more precise rendering seems in order. All Scriptural quotations are from the English Revised Version, unless otherwise stated.

I am grateful to Penguin Books Ltd. of London for permission to quote from Mr R. S. Pine-Coffin's translation of St. Augustine's *Confessions*.

Doubleday and Company kindly granted permission to quote from *Protestant-Catholic-Jew* by Will Herberg.

George Braziller, Inc. kindly granted permission to quote from Bernard Frechtman's English translation (copyright 1964) of Jean Paul Sartre's *The Words*.

R. H. A.

iv

Contents

Abbreviations: Sources Cited

CAMUS

CE   *Essais*, Bibliothèque de la Pléiade
CF   *The Fall*, tr. Justin O'Brien. Random House
CM   *Myth of Sisyphus*, tr. Justin O'Brien. Random House
CP   *The Plague*, tr. Stuart Gilbert. Random House
CR   *The Rebel*, tr. Anthony Bower. Random House
CS   *The Stranger*, tr. Stuart Gilbert. Random House
CT   *Théâtre, Récits, Nouvelles*. Bibliothèque de la Pléiade

GIDE

GW   *Les Cahiers et les poésies d' André Walter*. NRF. Gallimard

KIERKEGAARD

KF   *Fear and Trembling*, tr. Walter Lowrie. Doubleday

LA ROCHEFOUCAULD

RO   *Oeuvres Complètes*. Bibliothèque de la Pléiade

SAINT AUGUSTINE

SC   *Confessions*, tr. R. S. Pine-Coffin. Penguin Books (London)

SAINT-EXUPERY

SO   *Oeuvres Complètes*. Bibliothèque de la Pléiade
SV   *Vol de Nuit*. Gallimard

SARTRE

SH   *Huis Clos*. Gallimard
SN   *La Nausée*. Gallimard
SW   *The Words*, tr. Bernard Frechtman. Fawcett Publications

SCHOLARS

BC   Brée, Germaine. *Camus*. Harcourt, Brace & World, Inc.
BV   Brée, Germaine (ed.). "Camus," in *Twentieth Century Views*. Prentice Hall.
BH   Bédier et Hazard. *Littérature Française*. Vol. II. Larousse
BF   Bruce, F. F. *The Spreading Flame*. Paternoster Press
HP   Herberg, Will. *Protestant, Catholic, Jew*. Doubleday
MM   Mumford, Lewis. *The Condition of Man*. Harcourt, Brace

I

That Which is Spiritual

F.ew words are used more loosely today than the word *spiritual*. With some it has become almost synonymous with 'hidden' so that any emotion aroused by a work of art, a concert of classical or popular music, a religious experience, or an experience induced by drugs or transcendental meditation can fall within its province.

Camus is much more specific than this. He distinguishes between a realm of "vague nostalgias" on the one hand and "a desire for unity . . . a need for clarity and cohesion" on the other. (CM, 38) Gide in *Les cahiers d'André Walter* draws a similar distinction. Whenever André speaks of Emmanuèle's inner life it is to speak of her spirit, whereas when he speaks of his own it is of his soul. Seeking to win and possess her, he plays on her soul and, although it sometimes seems as if he is about to succeed, as on the night when he plays Chopin on the piano while she listens on the terrace just outside the window, yet her spirit always triumphs in the end. "I knew," sighed André, "that your spirit stole your soul away from me even though your soul longed for me." (GW, 74)

Saint-Exupéry defines most helpfully that which is spiritual. "The spirit does not occupy itself with things but rather with the sense or meaning which ties them together—it is another face which lies back of them. The spirit passes directly from full and open vision to absolute blindness."

The word *esprit*, translated 'Spirit' here, has a wide variety of

1

meanings in French literature ranging from the 'the mind' or 'intellect' to the 'Spirit'. It is quite clear that, in this particular quotation, Saint-Exupéry means the latter. To establish this, it is perhaps as well that I quote the passage more fully.

"I am struck by a fact which no one acknowledges: the life of the Spirit is intermittent, it comes and goes. The life of the Intelligence, it alone is permanent, or more or less so. There are very few variations in my faculties of analysis. The Spirit does not occupy itself with things but rather with the sense or meaning which ties them together—it is another face which lies back of them. The Spirit passes directly from full and open vision to absolute blindness." In the very next paragraph Saint-Exupéry continues: "Commandant Alias passed the night with the General discussing pure logic. Pure Logic! That is just what ruins the life of the Spirit." (SO, 275)

By contrast, the soul can be defined as the seat of the emotions which, if unbridled, govern the attitudes and actions of the one they inhabit. The spirit is deeper. If clear and enlightened it will harness, contain, and direct the unpredictable soul. Should some issue arise, however, to which the soul is particularly vulnerable, and should the soul break loose on this point, then the spirit will withdraw and vanish leaving the soul to indulge itself, exploring its potential. It is this latter state which fascinated Gide.

This brief preliminary discussion of the distinction between soul and spirit places at once in our hands the key to Camus's first book, *L'Envers et L'Endroit*. This little work, which many feel to contain the essence of all that is to follow, is simply the depicting of the awakening of spiritual consciousness. The book consists of a series of episodes, the first being a dinner party to which a young man has been invited. In the household there is an old lady who had formerly poured out to him her loneliness and sense of need in her old age. The old lady would frequently resort to prayer, to the comfort of her rosary, of her leaden figure of Christ and of her plaster statue of Joseph and the child which was all she had left when abandoned by her relatives. During the meal she sits alone behind the young man in the shadows—the food would have been too heavy for her at night. There is an amusing film showing at the local cinema and they decide to extend the evening by going to see it—the old lady would not be taken along because she would not be able to understand; she would be left alone in the apartment. The

moment of parting is most embarrassing for the young man who had sympathized with the old lady and had received her confidence. They shake hands and she does not want to let him go. He experiences pity for her and, paradoxically, for an instant, a violent hatred—it even enters his mind to "hit her as hard as he could." (CE, 17) Once in the street he is overcome momentarily by a sense of remorse. That which is spiritual about him is his ability sufficiently to abstract himself from the emotions of his soul in order to see himself clearly. He observes the enigmatic phenomenon of the almost simultaneous presence within himself of sympathy and hatred—that observation is spiritual. He sees 'L'Envers et L'Endroit', both sides of the coin. He has awoken to a consciousness, deeper than either or both, which is illuminating; it is the "other face which lies back of things" of Saint-Exupéry. The remainder of this first work is a series of similar instances of spiritual enlightenment where the relationship between two facets is perceived. The love of life and the disgust for it. The despair of life which leads to the love of it. The poverty of Camus's family, yet the riches of the North African sun. The preface, which he wrote many years later, is likewise filled with similar couples.

Meursault of *The Stranger* shows the same kind of spiritual enlightenment when he horrifies his spiritually unenlightened lawyer by saying: "all healthy beings at one time or another wish that those they love were dead." (CT, 1170) Love imprisons and restricts the one who is caught by it and, in those moments when the emotion is more or less dormant and hence the restriction more than usually apparent, there will naturally arise the desire to break loose. The lawyer becomes most agitated when Meursault speaks in this way and makes him promise never to say anything of the sort in front of the court or before the examining magistrate. He is only concerned with what will serve the case and such naïvely frank statements from his client might spoil everything. Meursault, on the other hand, didn't particularly mind if he was well represented or not and, when the lawyer left in a huff, would have liked to have held him back "to explain to him that all I wanted was his sympathy, not for him to make a better job of my defense but simply, if one could put it that way, unaffectedly as a friend." (CT, 1171) The 'other face which lies back of things' will be an embarrassment to those who are occupied with presenting a case, selling an idea; it

will be palatable only to those who can afford to be honest, real, true.

This is Caligula's main dispute with his patricians. Whenever they speak to him they say what they think is the most likely to put them in his good books—he discerns this and despises it. In their fear for their lives they seem totally ignorant of the fact that he loves the simple openness of Scipion and respects the partial forth-rightness of Cherea. There is a comic incident when two of their number, being told by Caesonia that Caligula is dying having vo-mited blood, respond each in the way he thinks will best serve his private cause. "Almighty God," says one, "I solemnly swear that, if he recovers, I will give two hundred thousand sesterces to the State Treasury." (CT, 92) "Oh Jupiter!" says the other, "Take my life in exchange for his!" Little did they know that Caligula had slipped onto the scene and overheard all that was said. "I accept your offer" he says to the first patrician "my treasurer will call by your house to pick up the money tomorrow." "You cannot know how much I am moved; this must mean that you love me?" he enquires of the other with hidden sarcasm. "Ah Caesar!" comes the gullible reply, "There is nothing that I wouldn't give on your behalf right here and now." "Take him away!" says Caligula to his guards. "But where are they taking me?"—"To your death, of course. You have given your life for mine!"

When Camus sees the absurd it is likewise in terms of both sides of the coin. There are relationships in *The Stranger* which are real and true as between Meursault and Celeste, Marie, Salamano, or even Raymond. On the other hand there are relationships which are simply formal play-acting, playing the game required by the structure of society. Some characters are wholly unreal, whereas a few oscillate between the two as in the case of the janitor of the Old People's home in the court scene when he is cornered and has to make a public stand one way or the other. On the individual plane there is the rational seeing of the absurdity of life: "Men die and they are not happy" says Caligula (CT, 16); and on the other side of this coin there is the spiritual nostalgia that this absurdity provokes: "This longing to solve, this need for clarity and cohe-sion." (CM, 38) The exposition is clear, unexaggerated, and true; it is the simple presentation of the spiritual state of man and his so-ciety.

When Sartre treats this same subject of the absurd, the outcome is different and the difference between the two further elucidates the spiritual nature of Camus's approach. To Sartre, absurd is a secondary word—"The word absurd takes shape at this moment at the point of my pen" he says, towards the end of his book *Nausea*—"Absurdity, it is not just an idea of my head. . . . it is this long dead serpent at my feet, this wooden serpent"—he is talking of a root of a tree! (SN, 182) He is dealing with the same subject as Camus but the primary impression he receives is that of Nausea. 'Absurd' expresses a dispassionate objective observation, 'Nausea' an emotional and probably physical involvement. Anyone can at any time, if he wishes to be honest, discern the absurdity of life; special circumstances and a willingness to go along with an inward malaise are necessary, however, to plumb the depths of 'Nausea'. A healthily occupied person who has to work for his living and, in his free time, enjoys the natural pleasures of life will be most unlikely to experience 'Nausea'. The ideal candidate is a Roquentin in his early or middle twenties with just enough money not to have to work for a living and whose sole occupation, which he can take up or drop as he pleases, is writing a thesis on a long-forgotten, rather uninteresting M. de Rollebon.

There is another distinction between Camus's characters' coming to see and understand the absurd and Sartre's Roquentin and his Nausea. The former effortlessly see that life and society are so, whereas the latter has to apply himself to the sensation he has received and voluntarily immerse himself in it if he is to grasp it; and his sensation is mainly preoccupied with things. "I musn't let the shades of meaning escape me, the little things, even if they don't seem to have any significance, and I must classify them. I must express *how* I see that table, the street, the people, my tobacco pouch since *that* is what has changed. I must determine the precise extent and nature of this change." (SN, 9) Camus's characters make an objective spiritual observation whereas Roquentin is obsessed with a change of sensation within himself in relation to some object which has not changed.

Furthermore, the spiritual understanding of Camus's characters is a constant—they have discovered what *is*; their perception may deepen but it does not come and go. Of course, should they be overcome by some emotion of the soul, for the time being their

spirit "would pass from full and open vision to absolute blindness"; but an experience of this sort would only serve to teach such a one as Jean Tarrou not to get caught that way again: He, Tarrou, and **Dr. Rieux** of *The Plague* seem to be men with spiritual X-ray eyes—they see through the surface of people and life in general. On the other hand, Roquentin can never tell when Nausea will attack him next—it comes over him without any forewarning at the most surprising moments and its sickening influence can almost paralyze him.

The real soulical nature of Nausea (and here I must coin a word **in English to translate the** Greek adjective psuchikos, the counterpart of spiritual—pneumatikos) can be perceived by examining the relationship between Roquentin and Anny. Up till their final meeting towards the end of the book, it had always been an ultraromantic affair, and romanticism is exclusively of the soul. It is rightly called 'le mal du siècle'—a kind of sickness. Rousseau's St. Preux and Julie of *La Nouvelle Heloïse* positively wallow in it until she is cured by her marriage to the level-headed M. de Wolmar and the subsequent healthy preoccupation with a growing family. Poor St. Preux, who does not have enough to do to fill his life, falls prey to his unhealthy nostalgias. It is difficult to tell whether he really wants to be cured or whether he prefers to cling to this pain in his soul as giving at least some meaning to life, providing him with a kind of morbid introverted joy born of self-pity.

Anny's was an aesthetic form of Romanticism. She carried with her an assortment of exotic shawls, mantillas, Japanese masks, and certain books and nick-nacks; wherever she went she set up the room of her dreams. She would always occupy a certain chair in a certain position in relation to the window and she would manipulate the conversation and atmosphere to produce a 'moment parfait', just as an actor, by word and gesture, methodically leads up to a climax. It was a world of her fantasy which she had dreamed up and lived out and which Roquentin was happy to share with her when she permitted.

The pendulum swings and one extreme will be followed by the other; it is no chance that the Realism of the 19th Century was the reaction to the sickly Romanticism of the late 18th and early 19th. Thus both Anny and Roquentin, when the dream ran out, found their souls swing to the opposite extreme of an earthy

realism which, in its preoccupation with tangible things, carried with it another sickness, not aesthetic and of the dream world this time, but of disgust and horror at the earthiness of the things themselves. The same things which served as symbols in a world of fantasy now provoked revulsion in the real. The things had not changed but there had been an enormous swing in the souls of those who were handling them.

I served at sea in the British Navy throughout World War II. The awfulness of that war was somewhat alleviated by the strong romantic element in the atmosphere. The British people was like a team with a united soul to win and Churchill officiating at the "pep rallies." How much harder for those in Vietnam—just stark realism, unrelieved. After the war I went as a student to Oxford University and, with the romantic drama of the conflict behind me, I too experienced the swing of the soul to naked realism and the nauseating feeling it conveys. Happily I soon recognized it as a malady and, whenever it reared its ugly head, whatever the weather, used to don my running clothes and go for a good long run along the towpath of a disused canal which, passing close by my college, led out into the country. A hot shower afterwards and a cup of tea completed the cure.

The starting point for Camus is with all these soulical flights of fancy discerned, categorized and deliberately rejected. "I hold certain facts from which I cannot separate" he writes. "What I know, what is certain, what I cannot deny, what I cannot reject —this is what counts. I can negate everything of that part of me that lives on vague nostalgias, except this desire for unity, this longing to solve, this need for clarity and cohesion. I can refute everything in this world surrounding me that offends or enraptures me, except this chaos, this sovereign chance, and this divine equivalence which springs from anarchy. I do not know if this world has a meaning which transcends it. But I do know that, if such a meaning exists, I do not know it and that it is impossible for me just now to know it." (CM, 38)

How perfectly this fits in with what the Apostle Paul has to say, in the second chapter of his first Epistle to the Corinthians, as to the nature and limitations of man. I quote from the translation by J. B. Phillips, taking the liberty to use the word 'soulical' where it (psuchikos) appears in the Greek. "For who could really under-

stand a man's inmost thoughts except the spirit of the man himself? How much less could anyone understand the thoughts of God except the very Spirit of God? And the marvelous thing is this, that we now receive not the spirit of the world but the Spirit of God Himself, so that we can actually understand something of God's generosity towards us. It is these things that we talk about, not using the expressions of the human intellect but those which the Holy Spirit teaches us, explaining spiritual things to those who are spiritual. But the soulical man simply cannot accept the matters which the Spirit deals with—they just don't make sense to him, for, after all, you must be spiritual to see spiritual things. The spiritual man, on the other hand, has an insight into the meaning of everything, though his insight may baffle the man of the world."

There are thus to Paul three levels of understanding. First there is that of the unspiritual man who lives, for the most part, as do the higher animals entirely, in the emotions of his soul. Then there is the man who is fully awakened to the spirit of the man within him who, by keeping counsel with this human spirit, has access to the "other face which lies back of things" which frees him from being side-tracked by the transitory emotions of the soul. Thirdly come those who, having received the Spirit of God, enter into an understanding of the things of God which would otherwise have been impossible for them to conceive. It is most interesting to observe that Camus saw clearly the distinction between the first two categories. He says he didn't know if the third existed: "I don't know if this universe has a meaning which transcends it. But I do know that, if such a meaning exists, I do not know it and that it is impossible for me just now to know it." He uses the word 'impossible' recognizing that, if such an ultimate meaning to the universe did exist, he lacked the faculty to comprehend it. But he qualifies this by ' . . just now. . ', thereby leaving the door open both to the possibility of there being such a meaning somewhere and this being possibly communicable to him at some time in the future through some faculty or medium of which he hitherto had no experience.

The Spiritual Quest in History

The study of any discipline leads sooner or later to history. Causes and effects are perceived which, having been the experience of one generation, become part of the knowledge upon which subsequent generations base their quest for progress and security. Ecologists, economists, population experts, medical men, and scientists all make their contributions to the general understanding. History in its totality, however, is but partly the inexorable, step by step, out-working of scientific discovery; there is another ingredient—the use man makes of this development, of the scientific discoveries and inventions entrusted to him. The philosophic historian seeks to explain this latter, rather unpredictable aspect—the reasons which cause man to change his attitudes and ways. In measure, even this latter is often explicable from the economic and social standpoint. The French Revolution, for example, can largely be explained as a reaction on the part of the peasants to the intolerable inequities imposed upon them for generations by the absolute, corrupt, and unjustly applied power of Louis XIV and his successors. There is no doubt, however, that this is not the whole story. The two and a half centuries which preceded the Revolution had seen such dramatic changes in spiritual outlook and such a leap in confidence in human reason that man would no longer submit himself, through super-stitious fear, to a religious political hierarchy for which he had lost respect. The economic and political circumstances, together with the

9

spiritual and philosophical climate, all combined to make revolution inevitable.

Man is a spiritual being with a sense of destiny and thus, back of all else, yet interwoven into the very warp and woof of the totality of history, there runs the thread of the aspirations of his heart. His spiritual history in the West can be traced in two separate ways neither of which, in isolation, gives an adequate presentation —there is the history of the church itself on the one hand and, on the other, the appraisal of the philosophers and freethinkers as to the influence of Christianity and the validity of its practices in different eras. Thus Arnold Toynbee, the famous British historian, called Communism the offspring of a twisted abnormal Christianity and Nietzsche, as quoted by Camus, said that "Socialism is only a degenerate form of Christianity." (CR, 69) Camus himself wrote: "Metaphysical rebellion, in the real sense of the term, does not appear, in coherent form, in the history of ideas until the end of the 18th Century—when modern times begin to the accompaniment of the crash of falling ramparts." (CR, 26) In this he, Camus, delves deeper than the other two in observing that, back of the radical change of thought seen in the advent of Marxism, it must be deduced that there had been a metaphysical rebellion which had long brewed in the turmoil of man's spirit before the day when it finally took coherent form in ideas. The purpose of this chapter is to delineate the principal surges of change of direction spiritually during the past two thousand years and to analyze the climate of the day in which Camus wrote.

Historically, the spiritual quest has two directions. Man has sought on the one hand to discover the truths of God and, on the other, the truths or principles which produce a happy state in society. These two directions, the vertical and the horizontal, were combined into one by Jesus Christ.   ,

"Master, what shall I do to inherit eternal life?" asked a lawyer. The reply he received was in the form of a question: "What is written in the law?" "Thou shalt love the Lord thy God with all thy heart and with all thy soul and with all thy strength and with all thy mind, and thy neighbor as thyself" replied the lawyer. His answer was evidently complete for he received the affirmation: "This do and thou shalt live." (*Luke*, 10.25)

To early Christians, life in the Church was the way to the fulfil-

ment of the quest, a society living together under God. There were doubtless few who thus analysed their position but, in fact, what they sought was the fulfilment of the vertical and the horizontal together in the realisation of the meaning of Immanuel—"God with us." In the early days it is evident that a form of communal life was practiced in which "the multitude of them that believed were of one heart and soul: and not one of them said that aught of the things which he possessed was his own; but they had all things common." (*Acts*, 4.32) Even if this practice did not continue for long, it is abundantly clear through the rest of the New Testament that a genuine love and concern existed amongst believers, holding them together and making them willing to lay down their lives for one another and the cause which had captivated them.

Under persecution the church thrived as has since been the case repeatedly throughout history; but, when Constantine attributed his victory at the Milvian bridge to the God of the Christians, the situation changed radically. Relieved to be able to enjoy the full rights of citizenship in the Roman Empire, the leaders of the Church went overboard in their gratitude to the Emperor and gave him a say in the internal affairs which was not properly his. At the council of Nicaea in 325 A. D. he was even permitted to preside as a kind of overseer over the bishops. "It was a fatal mistake," writes the French historian Palanque "and the two powers (Church and state) were destined to suffer long from its unfortunate consequences. Thus the church was scarcely freed from the oppression of its persecutors when it had to encounter a trial more terrible perhaps than that of hostility: the embarrassing and onerous protection of the State." (BF, 301)

What had been a simple spiritual family, driven to spiritual reality by persecution, became organised, accepted, and respected. A hierarchy quickly came into being whose power and domination increased rapidly until Europe bowed before its throne. Yet, for the average Christian of those days, what was life? Some faith, no doubt, but a great deal of superstitious fear. The cathedral stood not only at the geographical center of the city but was also the focus of all aspects of the life of the citizens. The clergy were the final authority on any subject they chose to pronounce upon. It was no longer Immanuel—"God with us"—but the clergy telling us what God would have us believe and do!

Was it this tightly constricted atmosphere which caused men in those days to become mystics? Was it because they were convinced of their impotence to change the order of things in the hierarchy and feudal system that they shut themselves off from society and sought God all alone? There have been mystics in every age but perhaps more in the Dark and Middle Ages. Maybe the 'why' is unanswerable, but that they sought thus, secluded from society and cloistered unto God, is fact. They sought through prayer and meditation and sometimes severe discipline to grow in their understanding of God and in sanctification—the subduing of their natural lusts and appetites and the transforming of their characters. Was it in despair of ever attaining any satisfaction along the lines of "God with us" that they narrowed their basis, abandoned the horizontal, and devoted themselves exclusively to the vertical and individual "God with me"? Their writings are beautiful and filled with longings for holiness, but the effect they produce is either to make the reader long likewise to escape from the world and its occupations or to produce in him a sense of inadequacy. There is something slightly unhealthy about the vertical when it is that and that alone. As someone so aptly put it—it is indeed possible to be so heavenly minded that one is no earthly good! The horizontal is a healthy discipline and check. The earth is earthy, and man often provokes that which is earthy in his neighbor, but the discipline of day-by-day encounter with it has the very salutary effect of keeping the feet solidly on the ground!

The Reformation rocked the hierarchical boat but the effect of the writings of Montaigne, though not immediately apparent, was to be fundamental, touching the very root and source of Christianity, namely revelation. He asked his question: "Que sçais-je?" (What do I know?); but the hidden question, implicit in the general tenor of his writings, is far deeper. At the heart of his work, his essays, appears his apology for Raymond Sebond in which he doffs his cap perfunctorily to Christianity and the principle of revelation whilst all the time giving the central place to Pyrrho, the founder of the school of philosophy—Pyrrhonism, and his systematic doubt. Montaigne is the timeless sceptic who is saying not so much "What do I know?" as "Is it possible for me to be sure that I know anything?"

It would be interesting to speculate on the emotions of Descartes as, having read Montaigne, he applied himself to set forth his *Dis-*

cours de la Méthode. Did he fear lest Montaigne's scepticism had opened a yawning gulf which would lead to anarchy and, as a countermeasure, propose a basis of reasoned thought as a substitute for revelation which was fast going out of fashion or did he simply regard Montaigne's writings as being the excuse he had been looking for to permit him to develop and proclaim his theorem of the sufficiency of reason? "Je pense donc je suis!" (I think and therefore I am) he wrote and, even though the adequacy of his formula was to be questioned in his day by such as Pascal and later proved false, nevertheless the door was opened for modern philosophy. Major scientific discoveries hastened one upon another in those days and Descartes's theorem gave to the scientifically minded the opportunity they were seeking to set aside spiritual considerations and deal directly and mathematically with ideas and knowledge. The spirit, Saint-Exupéry's that "other face which lies back of things," was deliberately left to one side in favor of scientific proof and the logical, methodical, reasoned comparison of ideas.

When Montesquieu published his *Spirit of the laws* it was as if a final lock gate had been opened and the torrent was loosed. Again, it was not so much what he wrote as the implication behind it all. The careful reader could not avoid the deduction that if indeed, as Montesquieu demonstrated, there is a spirit of the laws which operates irrevocably in societies according to their structure, be it despotic, monarchic, or republican, then God, having created this system, had subjected himself also to it with man. There was therefore no longer any need to seek Him: it was sufficient to seek out the laws themselves and how they operated, and then put them into practice in society.

The unholy trinity followed: Voltaire attacking objectively hypocrisy, unreality, and sham in the institutions; Diderot subtly seeking to prove subjectively the non-existence, or at least the non-essentiality of the spiritual or metaphysical realm; and finally Rousseau adding 'soul' and appeal to the movement. The Revolution was inevitable and, after it, the stage was set for the total rejection of the vertical in favor of a concerned effort to establish in the horizontal what the hierarchy had preached about for so long but failed hopelessly to produce. Unhappily there were instances of gross immorality within the priesthood; practices such as the selling of indulgences were exposed as indefensible and a grumbling disillu-

sionment turned into open revolt. Constantine had established a status quo in the horizontal which had driven seekers to the vertical alone—"God with me!" Now there was a spirit of change in the air. God was to be abandoned in the attempt to establish equality and justice amongst "us". It is both interesting and significant that some of the founders of the communist movement were theological students until, seeing the contradiction or the disparity between the thing taught and that practiced, in the act of revulsion against unreality, they rejected religion, God, and the very concept of a spiritual realm. Karl Marx summed it all up as an opium used by the ruling classes to dupe the masses and keep them in subjection.

Communism reached a peak of popularity amongst the avant-garde thinkers in Paris between the two world wars. Gide went to Moscow at the invitation of the Russians upon their hearing of his espousal of the communist cause. Malraux and Sartre were openly sympathetic to the movement and Camus actually became a member of the party for a few years until he discovered that this political movement, just like all others, had its moments of letting expediency govern rather than principle. The period immediately following the last war saw a change. If the 'threat' of communism still existed, the respect for it amongst the leading thinkers, as being a way by which Utopia might be ushered in, waned fast. The experience of Hungary and then Czechoslovakia finally convinced those who, till then, had still been willing to give the benefit of the doubt. It is the author's conviction that, should this civilization **have time enough ahead to permit the retrospective view,** history will mark these days as one more spiritual crisis—the point at which man became disillusioned with his efforts to establish the utopian society, "us".

It is just at this juncture that Camus wrote and articulated so clearly what the generation following the second world war was feeling. Caligula despairs of ever attaining the vertical, the moon; and of ever changing the horizontal, the society in which he lives. The return of youth to nature, the meteoric rise in the use of drugs as an escape into what is hoped may be a better world, the half-humorous title to a recent London musical show—"Stop the world, I want to get off"—all points to a kind of malaise. The revival of interest in the horoscope, astrology, spiritualism, demon worship, the occult, and Eastern mystical religion likewise indicates a groping

after a new direction. In his most enlightening book, *The Condition of Man*, Lewis Mumford, after tracing the hopes and fears of preceding generations, ends with a photograph of the dawn and affirms his conviction that the only hope is for some wholly new and hitherto unconceived direction to appear. "The foreground is dark, and it will become darker before the day breaks," he writes. "Nothing that is worth doing in our time will be done easily; that is, without a spiritual rebirth. Unless the blind recover their sight and the crippled learn to walk, our very knowledge will slay us." (MM, facing 407) History may well recognize Camus as one of its most eloquent and perceptive prophets of the end of an era who, whilst keeping a level head, succeeded in displaying incontrovertibly the plight of 20th century man, disillusioned with the vertical and the horizontal, casting about for some direction which might give meaning to his life.

3

Early Influences

I t was to the poor working-class section of Algiers that Catherine Camus brought her two infant sons shortly after her husband was killed at the battle of the Marne in the First World War. Here young Albert was to receive his first impressions which deeply influenced him and were to stay with him all his life. The apartment had but two rooms. Madame Camus and her sons shared it with a harsh domineering grandmother who was slowly dying of cancer and an uncle who was partially paralysed.

The early days were healthy ones as the young boy gave himself to the sports and swimming that were his delights. Before his first attack of tuberculosis in his teens, it was boxing and soccer which occupied him the most. He evidently became a somewhat proficient goalkeeper on the local soccer team. It is significant that he mentions Thursdays and Sundays as being the peak days of his week; on Thursdays he practised soccer and on Sundays he played in the matches. Thus, even at that age, he was quite uninhibited by any rule as to what one should or should not do on the Sabbath. In this his youth was quite opposite to that of Gide who, from his earliest conscious moments, felt himself to be incarcerated in a strait-jacket of Christian law which he felt he had to discard, as we read in *The Immoralist*, in his quest for freedom. Camus did not have to discard anything; he was able to approach the whole question of religion as he did any other, from the standpoint of a man who is

natural and free. In this he is Meursault of *The Stranger* although his interest in soccer delivered him from Meursault's opinion of Sunday: "I remembered that it was Sunday and that bored me: I do not like Sunday." (CT, 1137)

Providentially, one of his teachers in grade school took a deep interest in the boy and, working with him outside class time, prepared him for a scholarship which enabled him to proceed with his education in the High School of Algiers. Here he met Jean Grenier who, first as his High School teacher and later as his college professor at the University of Algiers, was to have a great influence upon the development of his thought.

"A Christian and something of a mystic" is the way Miss Germaine Brée describes Jean Grenier. (BC, 24) It was he who introduced Camus to Augustine and the church fathers, Pascal, Kierkegaard, and the moderns such as Gide; and doubtless it was at his instigation that Camus chose to write his philosophical thesis for his M.A. on the influence of Plotinus on Saint Augustine. This task necessitated a thorough study of the Bible, particularly the the New Testament, and the knowledge of scripture he gained at this time was never to be beyond beckoning distance in succeeding years. "If you are not familiar with the Scriptures I admit this won't help you," says Jean-Baptiste Clamence in *The Fall*. "But it does help you? So you know the Scriptures? Decidedly you interest me." (CF, 9)

But what was the religious outlook of this young student of Augustine? In his commentary on the M.A. thesis, Roger Quilliot says that Camus at this time regarded religion "as either an old woman's occupation, something to take your mind off when death is near; or the vague expression of youthful aspirations toward something greater than oneself, the obscure desire to find some reason for existence." (CE, 1220) He was a foreigner to the religious spirit and yet profoundly marked by metaphysical unrest, says Quilliot. Seemingly untouched by Christianity as he studied it objectively; nevertheless, at the same time, inwardly searching.

There is further indication of Camus's personal uninvolvement in religion at this time in his joining the communist party in 1934, just two years before the completion of his thesis. Did his studies confirm what was already a growing conviction of the sterility of the God-ward direction through religion? His subject, the compari-

son between the philosophies of the ancients and the doctrines developed in the early church to see what influence the former had on the latter, led him away from belief and even, at the conclusion of his paper, to ask the question: "Are there any notions which are properly Christian (original to Christianity)?" (CE, 1308) He concludes that, if history has done nothing to allay our fears as to the absence of originality in the concepts of the Gospel, one cannot but recognise in Christian thought "a kind of resonance which was more substantial than any the world had ever till then encountered." (CE, 1309) Analytically comparing doctrines with philosophies had a depressing effect upon him; but even this did not obliterate his spiritual sense that a certain note struck in Christianity differed from and outstripped all others in substance.

He must have turned to communism in the hope that man-ward there would be release for his pent-up inward desire for purposefulness, fulfillment, and the establishment of justice. This brief communist affiliation, just three years, was to be short-lived, however. An idealist with an inward spiritual quest will not long be happy in the international communist fold where principles are compromised to serve nationalistic ends. It was an incident of this sort, when through expediency the communist attitude toward the lot of the North African Arab was changed, which precipitated Camus's leaving the party. This crisis in his life betrays a fundamental attitude that was never to change and that later caused the rupture with Sartre. For him, Camus, the end never justified the means. The meaning of life was to be found in living itself, thus the means must justify themselves. A further comparison with Sartre, this time on the subject of revolt, helps greatly to clarify this.

In Sartre's *Les Mains Sales* (Dirty Hands), Hugo—the young aristocratic idealist revolutionary—is commissioned by one faction of the revolutionary party to liquidate the leader of the other faction, Hoederer, who is entering into political discussions with the Prince and the bourgeois regime to maneuver politically for the strongest possible position for the party after the country's imminent occupation by an enemy socialist state. After much procrastinating, because he grows to respect Hoederer, Hugo accomplishes his task and is put in jail for it. When he comes out it is to discover that the faction he served has changed its policy and adopted that of Hoederer—they tell him he must state that the murder was an

accident or motivated by jealousy if he wishes to avoid being liquidated in his turn; for, should he tell the truth, the party, now united, would lose the respect of the people. Hugo feels unable to comply with their demands because, if he were to do so, it would rob Hoederer historically of his true heroism. The play ends with the party members at the door of the apartment of their accomplice, Olga, who had sought to persuade Hugo to change his mind. "Nonrécuperable!" Hugo calls out to them—"Non-salvageable!" The thought, of course, is that there are occasions when 'dirty hands' are justifiable, even necessary, if they can achieve a desired political end. A Hugo, who will not compromise his principles for the good of the party, is an embarrassment which must be eliminated.

The Just Assassins is the title of Camus's play dealing with the same subject. He wrote it to demonstrate, in his own words, that "Justice is at the same time both an idea and an aspiration of the soul." He adds the plea: "Let us seek it from the human side without transforming it into this terrible abstract passion which has mutilated so many." (CE, 268)

The scene is set in Russia just prior to the Revolution. A group of revolutionaries are planning to kill the Grand Duke and amongst them are two very different characters, Yanek and Stepan. Stepan is an old hand at the game, a hardened revolutionary. He has been imprisoned and whipped for his loyalty to the cause and the effect has been to embitter him. He is a man dedicated wholly to reach one goal and to him any means is valid. But Yanek, Stepan says, is a poet and a revolutionary and you can't mix the two! He has a heart, and his heart is always getting in the way of his revolutionary ideals, confusing the issue! Stepan represents the naked ruthless idea, and Yanek the same idea but strongly tempered by the aspiration of the soul.

The day comes when the Grand Duke's carriage is to pass their way. Plans are made for a bomb to be thrown under it at a certain corner and it is decided that it is Yanek's turn to throw it. Yanek goes out with the bomb and the others wait in the apartment. They hear the carriage approach and pass without any explosion. Shortly after, Yanek comes in and, in tears, tells how he was all ready to throw the bomb when, at the last moment, he saw some children in the carriage with the Grand Duke and their serious and sad expression drained all the strength from him. Had they not been there, he

would joyfully have thrown the bomb, he says, but their presence took him by surprise and something in him held him back. Stepan flies into a rage and says that he knew all along that it was not safe to trust Yanek; a good revolutionary had to be dead to his emotions. Yanek, he says, should have gone ahead, no matter who was in the carriage.

The Grand Duke is due to pass by again in the near future, however, and the important matter is to decide who shall be entrusted with the bomb on this occasion. After a long discussion it is decided, much against the will of Stepan, to give Yanek a chance to redeem himself. This time the Grand Duke is alone, he throws the bomb, the carriage is blown up and there is a general feeling of relief that 'Yanek has succeeded!' However, this is but the beginning of his trials. Once in the prison he meets first of all another inmate, Foka, who had been convicted of committing murder during a wild brawl. Foka, however, is paying his way out by acting as prison hangman; each time he executes his function at the orders of the authorities, and hangs an accused man, his prison term is reduced by one year. "It's a good deal!" he says. Yanek is shocked: "Do you mean to say you have become an executioner?" he asks in amazement. "Well! What about yourself?" retorts Foka. (CT, 364) How hard for Yanek to have his idealistic revolutionary act called the deed of an executioner! But worse is to come in the person of Skouratov, a sort of Stepan who has relinquished the cause and joined the ranks of the secret police, a thief set to catch a thief. How Yanek has to battle to keep his heart in the control of his head! "I threw the bomb against your tyranny, and not at a man" he says. "Doubtless, but it was the man who got hit and it made quite a mess of him," says Skouratov. "Do you know, my friend, that when they found the body, the head was missing. It had gone completely, and, as for the rest of him, only an arm and a bit of one leg were recognisable!" (CT, 366)

Finally the Grand Duke's wife comes into the cell. (I should mention that this play is taken almost to the detail from an incident which actually occurred in Russia.) She says that she wants to forgive Yanek and wants to ask God and man to forgive him too. But he refuses to accept a forgiveness that would nullify his revolutionary act and insists on paying for the death of the Grand Duke by his own in order for his conscience to be clear. She goes further

and says that she wants him to pray with her; but, down the narrow
course he is treading, forgiveness from man or prayer to God would
be compromise. "I feel nothing but compassion for you," he says.
"You have touched my heart. You will understand me now for I
shall hide nothing from you. I am no longer looking forward to a
meeting with God. In dying, I shall be right at the rendezvous that
I have made with those whom I love, my brothers who are thinking
about me at this moment. To pray would be to betray them." The
pain must, if possible, have worsened when the Grand Duchess told
him that her husband was just such a man as he—he was always
talking about justice and was so friendly with his workmen whereas the two children, at whom Yanek had refused to throw the bomb,
were not like that at all. "My niece has an unpleasant nature," said
the Grand Duchess "she refuses to carry her alms to the poor herself. She is frightened of being soiled by touching them." (CT, 373)

The other revolutionaries, knowing what is going on, wait anx-
iously to see if Yanek will be strong enough to see it through. It is
a relief when the day comes for his execution and he goes to the
scaffold unflinchingly. What is the overall impression the reader
is left with? A sense of desolation! Stepan was dead to anything
but the naked idea of Justice from before the beginning of the
play—the conflict centered around Yanek. In one sense he succeeded in that he went through with his determination; but in
another he failed because, in order to 'succeed', he had to act as
Stepan would have acted and this was only possible through his
making a continual effort to silence and stifle in himself that other
side of Justice—the aspiraton of the soul. Stepan had become so
embittered that he could no longer be hurt; that other side of him
was dead. Yanek, on the other hand, remained living and vital, yet
'mutilated' by the 'abstract passion.'

Before the throwing of the bomb there is a little scene in which
Yanek talks with Dora, the one female member of the party. They
love one another but realise that this love too must be sacrificed for
the cause. "We are not of this world" says Dora. "We are the Just
Ones. Oh! how pitiable is the lot of the just ones!" (CT, 353)
"Yes! that is our lot," says Yanek. "For us love is impossible."
There is a nobility about their willingness to sacrifice, yet it is a
tragic nobility as there is a deep sense of waste in it all. The
play never questions the validity of the cause but it proves without

question, to the sympathetic reader, that the means used to that end are wrong. Caligula finally has to admit that the way he has gone about seeking to establish truth in society is not the right one. "I did not take the route that I ought to have taken; I have accomplished nothing," he says. (CT, 108) The reader of *The Just Assassins* is spared the agony of Yanek and Dora coming to the same conclusion after it is too late.

This aspect of justice which Camus called "an aspiration of the soul" forms the very essence of the stimulus behind his works. Some have called it a sense of moral conciousness, I prefer to call it spiritual awareness. After all, had Camus recognised the distinction between the terms soul and spirit, as described in the first chapter, he would surely have regarded this "aspiration", which was a constant, as being an attribute of the spirit rather than belonging to the realm of the "vague nostalgias" of the soul. One final comparison with Sartre will serve to clarify even more the idea-dominated Stepan in the one and the spiritually aware Yanek in the other.

In his recent book *The Words*, Sartre recounts for us three spiritual experiences which were fundamental to his arriving at his present philosophical position. The first occurred in his childhood and came upon him unawares: "Only once did I have the feeling that He (God) existed. I had been playing with matches and burned a small rug. I was in the process of covering up my crime when suddenly God saw me. I felt his gaze inside my head and on my hands. I whirled about in the bathroom, horribly visible, a live target. Indignation saved me. I flew into a rage against so crude an indiscretion, I blasphemed, I muttered like my grandfather: 'God damn it, God damn it, God damn it.' He never looked at me again." (SW, 64) Speaking a little later of this incident, he adds somewhat cynically: "Whenever anyone speaks to me about Him today, I say, with the easy amusement of an old beau who meets a former belle: 'Fifty years ago, had it not been for that misunderstanding, that mistake, the accident that separated us, there might have been something between us.' "

The second and third experiences were more in the form of decisions which he made and then acted upon. The second: "One morning in 1917, in La Rochelle, I was waiting for some schoolmates with whom I was to go to the lycée. They were late. After a while, not knowing what else to do to occupy my mind, I decided to

think of the Almighty. Immediately he tumbled into the blue and disappeared without giving any explanation. He doesn't exist, I said to myself with polite surprise, and I thought the matter was settled." (SW,157) The third occasion, more far-reaching and drastic in its consequences, is recounted briefly and simply: "I collared the Holy Ghost in the cellar and threw him out; atheism is a cruel and long-ranged affair: I think I've carried it through." (SW, 158)

It is not difficult to imagine anyone having the second of these experiences. Trying to conjure up in one's imagination a picture of the Almighty God would have very similar effects, no matter who tried it, unless the attempt was accompanied by some mystical or psychological inducement. The other two occasions are different, however, and much more serious. They represent the deliberate putting to death of an inward aspect of the man, the cutting off of a consciousness. Here again is the basic difference between Sartre and Camus, between Stepan and Yanek. There is a verse in the Scriptures which has puzzled theologians for many generations but which the above does much to clarify. "Every sin and blasphemy shall be forgiven unto man, but blasphemy against the Holy Spirit shall not be forgiven. And whosoever shall speak a word against the Son of Man, it shall be forgiven him. But whosoever shall speak against the Holy Spirit, it shall not be forgiven him neither in this world nor in that which is to come." (Matthew, 12.31-2) It is one thing to speak against God objectively, or even against His Son; but inwardly and subjectively to repulse the voice of the Spirit and to sever relations with Him results in a kind of spiritual death which is irreparable; and Sartre says that that is what he has sought to do himself. Camus, on the other hand, says that he cannot believe in God objectively but never do we find any indication of an inward rejection of spiritual consciousness in him; in fact we find just the opposite. I am glad that the Scriptures affirm that any objective statements we make are forgivable; there is something **awful, final and disastrous**, however, about Sartre's defiant account of his violent expulsion of the Holy Spirit. When asked what he thought of his young relative's success in being awarded the Nobel prize for literature, the late Albert Schweitzer said that he was delighted. When the questioner went further and asked: "But what about his being an atheist?" Schweitzer evidently replied: "Oh!

God will forgive him for that!" There is surely an issue in all this which cannot be brushed aside that easily!

Why should the Scriptures affirm that this inner rejection of the Holy Spirit is unforgivable? Is it because such an act represents a measure of rebellion beyond the point that God will tolerate? Surely not! According to the Scriptures, and Camus came to realise this by experience, man can do nothing to improve his nature. In his preface to *The Two Sides of the Coin* he writes: "As has everyone, so have I tried to correct my nature by applying morality to it. It is this, alas, which has proved to be the most difficult thing for me. With a great effort, and I have made such, one can manage sometimes to conduct oneself in accordance with morality, but never to be it." (CE, 11) If that inward thread, lifeline, of the Spirit is broken there is no more hope of the man, as to his nature, being changed for the better. A redeeming feature of the mock trial of President Johnson conducted in Sweden under the sponsorship of Sartre and the late Bertrand Russell is that, quite apart from whatever might be his opinions on the Vietnam conflict, there is evidently still alive in Sartre, despite himself, an aspiration towards justice and a desire to appeal to man's conscience. Judas went out and hanged himself, and that could be called a good sign too in the sense that it showed he was far from dead to what he had done.

So Camus says objectively that he cannot believe in God. But in this affirmation he is not strong as, in the next breath, he says that he does not like to be called an atheist. Dr. Rieux of *The Plague*, when asked by Jean Tarrou if he believes in God, replies: "No! But what does that mean? I am in the darkness and I am trying to see clearly and for a long time now I have realised that I am not the only one in this predicament." (CT, 1320) A few minutes later in the same conversation the Doctor says to Tarrou: "Perhaps it is better for God that one does not believe in Him and that one fights with all one's might against death without raising one's eyes towards the heavens where he remains silent." (CT, 1321) It is not so much that Camus does not believe in God as that he does not see how a God could tolerate a state of affairs in the world where children are tortured and innocence suffers. Thus, even as to the existence of God objectively, Camus is not strong in his negation. Someone once told me, I have never seen this in print anywhere, that, towards the end of his life, he replied in this way to the ques-

tion so frequently put to him as to whether he believed God existed: " No! I do not believe so, but I would happy to be proved wrong." There is no assurance of course that he said this, but it does seem quite the sort of thing which could have fallen easily from the lips of Dr. Rieux.

Discussing together well-known 20th century literary figures, a prominent critic said to the author: "The trouble with Sartre is that he has too many ideas whereas Camus has too few!" A thought-provoking statement, catchy in its conciseness but which nevertheless contains a flaw. Sartre had ideas but Camus observed principles of life. "I am not a philosopher," he said. "I know only how to speak of those things I have experienced." The paradox about Camus is that Christians reading his works have seen in them, more clearly portrayed than in most so-called Christian literature, the great principles of the spiritual state of man. The Dominicans of the monastery at Latour-Maubourg were so interested in his work that they asked him to visit and address them. Camus himself wrote in a letter in 1943: "I have some Catholic friends and for those amongst them who are real Catholics I have something beyond sympathy, I feel a common bond towards a common goal. The fact of the matter is that they are occupied with the same things as I." (CE, 1596) The common bond being the welfare both spiritual and physical of man.

The question naturally arises as to how Camus came to think like this; how did he arrive at these great principles? Any answer to this question would have to lean heavily on conjecture; there are certain facts and principles, however, which lend sufficient justification to such conjecture as to warrant their mention here. The relationship between Jean Grenier and Camus was close and of long standing, extending from his high school years through the completion of his M.A. thesis in college and thereafter for the remainder of his life. It is abundantly clear merely from the substance of his thesis that spiritual considerations played an important if not dominant role in the studies which these two shared. The nature of spiritual things is that first of all they are glimpsed either through something read or heard. The thing glimpsed may fade totally away but the seed remains and one day, perhaps years later after life experiences that illustrate and substantiate, comes illumination and understanding. The initial glimpse may have been long for-

gotten and the one who now sees fully and openly may feel that what he has arrived at is quite original with him. G. H. Lang, the well-known biblical scholar, tells how in his youth he read with great interest the works of the famous expositor, G. H. Pember. After a long time, during which his understanding of spiritual things developed widely, he reread the works of Pember and was amazed to discover (I believe I am quoting him correctly) "how much of my stock in trade I owed to him." Camus understood this principle. He observed that each man comes to see two or three great truths during his life but that it takes about ten years for him fully to possess one of them. Seeds were planted through the contact with Jean Grenier which developed in the life of Camus, the non-Christian, who later came to possess and fully perceive, in the life of man and society, things he had first heard from his professor and friend. It can likewise be said of Gide that the inspiration behind his literary work up to 1918 was the spiritual quality of the life of his wife—the talent and gift with words were his. Camus's extraordinary literary gift enabled him to make the principles and truths he had perceived accessible and understandable to anyone, of any religious persuasion or none, who was seeking, with an open spirit, to understand the plight of mid-20th century man. And now for the principles he brought to light.

4

The Absurdity of Life

There is a striking similarity between the thoughts of Sisyphus about the absurdity of life and the words of Solomon concerning vanity in Ecclesiastes. Both conclude that, from man's standpoint at least, life is a closed cycle with no evident purpose—"What profit hath man for all his labour . . . that which hath been is that which shall be; and that which hath been done is that which shall be done . . . . and there is no new thing under the sun" (Ecclesiastes, 1.1-9); but both also agree that there is contentment to be found in living—"There is nothing better for a man than that he should eat and drink, and make his soul enjoy good in his labour."

After the death of Drusilla, when Caligula returned from three days and nights in the open, he had received such a revelation of vanity and absurdity that contentment had become impossible for him. It is apparent that something drastic has happened, for his whole demeanor has changed. "I am not mad," he says, by way of explanation to his trusted servant Helicon. "In fact I have never been more level-headed. It is just that I have suddenly felt the need to attain something impossible. Things as they are no longer seem satisfactory to me." (CT, 15) "There are many others who feel just like that," replies Helicon. "That's true," says Caligula. "But I didn't know it before. Now I know. This world, as to its order, is intolerable to me now. So I need the moon or happiness or immortality, something which may sound crazy perhaps but which is not

of this world." He refuses to give in, compromise and come to terms with this vertical impasse yet recognizes he is impotent to accomplish anything in this directon. Assigning this less immediate task of resolving the vertical to Helicon, he hurls all his energies and authority as Emperor into seeking to establish reality and truth in society, the horizontal. Thus the play is a microcosm of the spiritual history outlined in the second chapter of this book. But this is to leap too swiftly to the conclusion.

"Men die and they are not happy," says Caligula (CT, 16); and he expresses so simply in practical terms the deadlock reached by the man who has seen vanity. Rupert Brooke evidently regards this understanding as being so general that even aquatic life shares it! He calls his poem *Heaven.*

> "Fish, fly-replete in depth of June,
> Dawdling away their watery noon,
> Ponder deep wisdom dark or clear
> Each secret fishy hope or fear.
> Fish say they have their stream and pond,
> But is there anything beyond.
> This life cannot be all they swear,
> for how unpleasant if it were,
> One may not doubt that somehow good
> Shall come of water and of mud.
> And sure the reverent eye must see
> A purpose in liquidity.
> We darkly know, by faith we cry
> The future is not wholly dry.
> Mud unto Mud—death eddies near—
> Not here the appointed end, not here!
> But, somewhere beyond space and time
> Is wetter water, slimier slime;
> And there, they trust, there dwelleth One
> Who dwelled ere rivers were begun,
> Immense of fishy form and mind,
> Squamous, omnipotent and kind.
> And under, that Almighty Fin,
> The littlest fish may enter in."

The difference between Rupert Brooke's fish and Caligula is that the former has faith in an Almighty fin whereas the latter,

having nothing but a question vertically, seeks to vent his conse-quent frustrations by forcing a change in those around him.

About ten years ago a movement arose in the private schools along the Eastern Seaboard of the United States which the parti-cipants called *Nihilism.* What had in effect happened was that the quest of Caligula had broken loose amongst the young students. Fortunately, however, in their case the quest was moderated by Sisyphus's philosophical contentment with living. In essence what they were saying was that they could not see any purpose in life, any objective. They tried the chapel and felt as empty as ever; nothing seemed to help. For a period this movement was a source of deep concern to the school administrators who found themselves powerless to do anything about it. The problem was the honesty of the students! They said that if at their age, late teens, they were offered a large sum of money to do something in the business world which, though not altogether wrong, was nevertheless not absolutely honest, they would not do it. But what frightened them was the thought that perhaps, in their early thirties, the pressures of life might drown their scruples and they might well invent excuses for themselves and go ahead and do the thing. They feared lest they might be tempted to compromise as had Cherea, a prom-inent political leader in the play *Caligula.*

"Something in me is just like what is in Caligula" said Scipion, the poet whom Caligula loves. "The same flame burns in each of our hearts." (CT, 83)

"Yes!" answers Cherea. "But there are times in a person's life when he must choose. I have chosen and have silenced and put to death in myself that thing which is like him."

Scipion has the same longing to penetrate beyond the absurd and vanity as does Caligula, but he is a poet. Like Yanek he cannot throw himself ruthlessly into seeking by any means to attain his end; in this he is unlike Caligula, who has a Stepan's determination. Cherea, however, is what one would call a practical man. He would say that idealism is all right in its place but that one should not let it run one's life because, after all, one has to live in this world. He is the man of good taste, the middle-of-the-road type whom Tarrou describes thus: "Good taste consists in not insisting on anything." (CT, 1422) His voice would not satisfy the young students of the Nihilism movement at all; but their fear is that it might seem

treacherously attractive later in life when they have a position in society and a family to educate! Germaine Brée writes: "A Caligula has lived perhaps more or less faintly in all of us and disappeared at the hands of an inner Cherea, Caligula's challenger, when we turned thirty." (BC, 153)

But does Camus accept that it is inevitable for Caligula and his determined spiritual aspiration towards reality to be put to death by the mediocre, security-loving Cherea? Not at all! There is surely a significance in the final curtain falling as Caligula cries out: "I am still alive!" (CT, 108) It is as if Camus is saying: do whatever one will, he is never altogether killable in any of us.

Frustrated in his quest for "the moon," Caligula turns to the society in which he lives. "All around me men are content to live in a lie of unreality whereas I long that we shall live in the truth." (CT, 16) As it seems to him that there is no God or man with the power and inclination to upset the status quo, Caligula decides to take the matter in hand himself. "I have the means of making them live in the truth because I know what they lack," he says to Helicon. "They are deprived of knowledge and what they need is a teacher who knows what he is talking about." (CT, 1153) All his efforts fail, of course; it is impossible to force anyone to live in the light of a spiritual verity he has not seen himself.

It is in *The Stranger* that the second aspect of the absurd, the horizontal, is seen the most clearly. The English translation of the title of this novel lacks force—the French word 'L'étranger' really means not so much 'The Stranger' as 'The Foreigner'; and this latter is precisely what the hero of the book, Meursault, finds himself to be. He is a foreigner in a world which doesn't understand him and in which he frequently has experiences which make him feel a misfit. Happily, however, there are some such as his girl friend Marie, Celeste the restaurant owner, old Salamano, Raymond, and his friend Masson with whom he enjoys simple sympathetic relationships. These people are not pretending to be something they are not, nor are they trying to attain some higher place in society. They have seen that there is more to life than so-called 'getting ahead'; but to try to explain this understanding to someone firmly ensconced in the absurd is quite a hopeless task, as Meursault finds when his boss offers him the opportunity of going to Paris to open up an office there.

"You are young," said my boss, "and I'm pretty sure you'd enjoy living in Paris. And, of course, you could travel about France for some months in the year."

"I told him that I was quite prepared to go; but really I didn't care much one way or the other.

"He then asked me if a 'change of life', as he called it, didn't appeal to me, and I answered that one never changed his way of life; one life was as good as another, and my present one suited me quite well.

"At this he looked rather hurt, and told me that I always evaded the issue and that I lacked ambition—a grave defect, to his mind, when one was in business.

"I returned to work. I'd have preferred not to vex him, but I saw no reason for 'changing my life'. By and large it wasn't an unpleasant one. As a student I had had plenty of ambition of the kind he meant. But, when I had to drop my studies, I very soon realised that all that was without any real importance." (CT, 115)

The meaning of life to these people is the enjoyment of their lot and the simple relationships they have with one another. They are not necessarily good; Meursault and Marie are just natural whereas Raymond is morally bad; but they are real, and they all have names! On the other hand, in the absurd, everyone seems, outwardly at least, to be morally good; but no one dares to be real, nor do they have names because you never meet the real person, just the role he is playing—the boss, the director of the old people's home, the examining magistrate, the prison chaplain, etc.! How similar to the Gospels where one group is formed, for the most part, of poor, sick, sinful, needy, or bad people who are real; and the other of correct, aloof, self-satisfied, nameless people—the Scribes, Pharisees, lawyers, chief priests and rulers—who are not really living at all themselves but just acting out the dictates of a religious code.

After the accident on the beach, when Meursault shoots the Arab, his lawyer visits him in his prison cell and the distinction between these two realms can be seen so clearly from their first conversation together.

"He was short and tubby, fairly young, with his hair carefully plastered in position. Despite the heat, I was just in shirt sleeves, he had on a dark suit, a stiff collar and an odd-looking black and white striped tie. He put on my bed the briefcase he had brought

under his arm, and introduced himself. He said that he had studied my case and that it was rather a tricky one. but that he had no doubt of success if I would just confide in him. I thanked him and he said, 'Right, let's get on with it!' "

"He sat down on my bed and explained to me that some enquiries had been made into my private life. They had discovered that my mother had died recently in the Old People's Home at Marengo and that they had made some enquiries there. They had learned that I showed a certain lack of sensitivity on the day my mother was buried. 'You understand', my lawyer added, 'That I really dislike having to ask you this kind of thing, but it is most important. It will be a strong point in favor of the prosecution if I don't have an answer to it'. He wanted to help me. He asked if I had been upset on that day. The question surprised me a lot, and it seemed to me that I would have been most embarrassed if I had to ask it of someone else. I simply replied that I had never really asked myself that question and thus it was difficult to reply. . . . One thing I could say for sure was that I would have preferred that my mother had not died. But the lawyer did not seem satisfied. 'That's not enough', he said. He thought for a moment and then asked if he could say that on that day I had suppressed and hidden my natural feelings. 'No!' I answered, 'because it's not true.' He looked at me oddly as if I had caused him a vague feeling of disgust, and then said nastily that, in any event, the director and the employees of the Old People's Home would be heard as witnesses and that that could go really badly for me. I pointed out to him that that incident had nothing to do with my case, and he simply replied that it was quite evident that I had never had dealings with the law.

"He was quite angry when he left. I would have liked to call him back, to explain to him that all I really wanted was his sympathy and understanding, not so that my case would be better defended but, for want of a better word, unaffectedly as a friend. I saw clearly that I upset him. He didn't understand me and was holding something against me. I longed to assure him that I was just like everybody else, just like everybody else." (CT, 1170)

There is something here beyond the naïvete and ingenuousness of Voltaire's Candide or L'Ingénu or Gide's Lafcadio; they were interesting to those around them and often arouse amused sympathy in the reader. Meursault, however, provokes disgust and

anger which are really no more than a cover-up for a guilty conscience in his lawyer. The issue is honesty and truth. Meursault may
be lazy, indifferent, and amoral in his outlook but he is completely
honest quite regardless of whether this may be an embarrassment
to others.

"In the evening, Marie came to fetch me," he recounts, "and
asked me if I wanted to marry her. I told her that I was quite agree-
able to the thought and that we could go ahead and do so if that
was what she wanted. She then asked me if I loved her. I answered,
as I already had once before, that it didn't really mean anything
but there was no doubt that I did not love her." (CT, 1154)

One may criticize him and ask how, if he did not love her, he
could justify his behavior towards her; but the honesty remains like
a burst of sunshine dispelling the shadows and exposing what
really is! Honest men, in this sense of the word, are somewhat rare.
How many, many young men will assure a girl they love her but,
when the subject of matrimony arises, will politely decline. How
interesting and enigmatical is a Meursault who, whilst willing to
accommodate his girl friend by marrying her, nevertheless tells her
quite openly he does not love her! But we must return to the history
of his court case.

When the day for the trial arrives, each character is forced to
choose to which realm he will publicly commit himself. Meursault
describes the atmosphere amongst the judges, lawyers, and news-
papermen as that of a kind of club in which he felt strangely out
of place. They greeted one another and congratulated each other
on their respective performances just as one would at a football
banquet, for example. On the other side, his friends said all they
could to persuade the jury of his innocence. There is a very
touching moment when Celeste tried to find words to express his
feelings, but without avail, and he is politely but firmly hurried up
by the judge. "Celeste turned and gazed at me. His eyes were
moist and his lips trembling. It was exactly as if he were saying:
'Well, I've done the best I could, old pal, I'm afraid it hasn't helped
much, I'm sorry.' I didn't say anything or make any movement, but
for the first time in my life I wanted to embrace a man." (CT,
1189)

In between these two extremes, however, there are some who
would like to show sympathy but do not dare. They are frightened

by the togetherness and sheer weight of the absurd. The janitor of the Old People's Home for instance has quite obviously been intimidated into saying all the prosecution wishes. "Replying to questions, he said that I had declined to see mother's body, that I had smoked cigarettes and drunk café au lait. . . . They got the janitor to repeat what he said about the cigarettes and the café au lait. . . . my counsel asked if he too had not smoked. . . . The prosecutor took strong exception to this. . . . nonetheless the judge told the janitor to answer the question. The old man fidgeted a bit. 'Well, I know I oughtn't to have done it', he mumbled, 'But I did take a cigarette from the young man when he offered it—just out of politeness.' The judge asked me if I had any comment to make. 'None,' I said, 'except that the witness is right. It's quite true that I offered him a cigarette.' The janitor looked at me with surprise and a sort of gratitude. Then, after hemming and hawing a bit, he volunteered the statement that it was he who had suggested that I should have some coffee!" (CT, 1187)

The uniting force of the absurd is a kind of fear—fear of losing position, acceptance, security, and a future of being left alone—and its motivating energy is pride, the lust to 'get ahead' of someone else and have the inward satisfaction of feeling a success in one's own context. The uniting force of the other realm is sympathy, love, and understanding. On encountering a person who is solidly ensconced in the absurd, a real person will have the impression of not making himself clear, of not being properly understood, and that he needs to explain or excuse himself. "I fixed up with my employer for two days' leave" says Meursault, asking to attend his mother's funeral. "Obviously, under the circumstances, he couldn't refuse. Still, I had the idea he looked annoyed, and I said, without thinking: 'Sorry sir! but it's not my fault you know!' Afterwards it struck me that I needn't excuse myself; it was really up to him to express his sympathy." (CT, 1125) The absurd man must be thick-skinned and insensitive to be able to continue bringing those who are foreigners to his realm under a sense of inadequacy and inferiority; but perhaps he is not so sure of himself as he seems, and beneath the absurd exterior foment the usual human fears and apprehensions!

Happily these two realms are not watertight compartments. There is at least one character in *The Plague* who, as a result of

suffering, moves from the one to the other. M. Othon is a prose-cuting magistrate and anyone making his acquaintance meets the magistrate and not the person. He has even begun to look like his role, tall, thin, and sombre: "All existence for a man turned away from the eternal is but a vast mine under the task of the absurd," says Camus (CM, 70); and M. Othon mimed the magistrate's part! But his son, the only son of his and his wife's old age, caught the plague. Finally the little boy dies and the suffering of this experience opens up M. Othon and he changes altogether.

At this point I cannot refrain from telling one or two experiences which came my way in the past war. Anyone who has seen action in a war has had a taste of the difference between the Absurd and what is real. "I honestly hope I shall not live through to peace time," said a Midshipman friend of mine aboard the battle cruiser *Hood*. "I couldn't bear to go back to that unreality and playing at life all over again. It would be intolerable!" He didn't go back to it, he went down with his ship when it sank after being hit by the German battleship *Bismarck*.

But there was another experience which seems almost incredible in retrospect. We put to sea from Malta in a submarine and set sail for the Aegean sea. After we had been at sea for about two days and had passed through various mine fields on our way to our patrol area, and naturally could not lightly return to harbor, a seaman came to me; he was bright red in the face and covered with spots. "I'm sick!" he said. "That's obvious!" I replied. When we took his temperature it was around 105 degrees; it was clear that he was seriously ill. "Why didn't you say something about this before now?" I asked him. "Did you know you were ill before we left harbor?" "Yes I knew!" he replied, "but I was frightened that if I said anything you might have left me ashore and then have gone off to sea yourselves and got sunk without me!"

In peacetime, when we are living what we call a normal life, this seems not only incredible but ridiculous; but that was the kind of atmosphere we lived in. We had been thrown together in ad-versity and danger to such a degree that we had come to know one another as real persons and to respect and have a genuine attach-ment for one another—we felt ourselves to be part and parcel of the ship and crew. We were drawn together and out of ourselves in devotion to a goal and enjoyed the priceless experience of deli-

verance from our individual selves and their littleness. Saint-Exupéry knew this too: "True love," he says, "consists not in looking at one another but in standing shoulder to shoulder and facing in the same direction." (SO, 252)

After the war I received a letter from a former crew member of a submarine. His peacetime occupation was sausage-making; he was quite a wealthy man—I recall that his wife came to wave him good-bye wearing what appeared to be a mink coat! His duty onboard was forward torpedo-man; he had to live in very cramped conditions in the bow and reload torpedos. "Sir, after to-day's heart-rending experience I must write to you," he wrote. "I was walking through Rosyth dockyard and I stepped on a metal plate and looked down, and it was the name-plate of our old submarine! Do you know that they have cut her to pieces and they're selling her for scrap? And it broke my heart!"

It sounds so sentimental but there is a great deal more to it than that. His mind had fled back to those days when together we entered hardship and danger, when our lives were in the balances and could have been snuffed out at any moment; and in those days we were real and touched a fraternity which many do not know even exists. Saint-Exupéry knew all about it and called it the only true luxury. No wonder he experienced an inner anguish as he looked upon droves of bureaucrats in each of whom there was "a little assassinated Mozart!" (SO, 261)

Happy the man who, in trials, has discovered inward values and depths both in himself and others which he never knew existed before. Gide came to understand this principle through reading Saint-Exupéry and coined a word for it—'surpassement de soi' —'going beyond yourself'. (SV, 10) There is a profound sense, not so much of achievement, as of having tapped a hidden and priceless source when individually Saint Exupéry's pilots overcome impossible odds—the incident when Guillaumet was lost for a week in the snow-covered mountains comes to mind. When the experience is shared, however, a link of fraternity is forged between those who share it which no other experience on this earth can match in depth.

In *The Plague* there is the same atmosphere amongst the medical groups organised by Tarrou and Dr. Rieux. Even Rambert, the journalist who is desperate to get out of the city and back to his

mistress in Paris, finally joins and then does not want to leave. Paneloux, the Jesuit Priest, joins too and M. Grand devotes what time he can to the work. Lastly, of all people, M. Othon, the prosecuting magistrate, comes and offers his services. No wonder Dr. Rieux notes that something must have changed. . . "could it be that a sudden gentleness showed in those hard, inexpressive eyes? Yes, they had grown misted, lost their steely glitter." (CT, 1429) The oyster must suffer to bring forth the pearl, carbon must experience great pressure to yield a diamond, a woman must travail to give birth to a child and, in the scripture, suffering and glory go hand in hand. Thus do tribulations and trials, which we all seek to avoid, often have the very salutary effect of shaking us out of the Absurd into the realisation of the existence of another and far better realm of reality, honesty, and sympathy.

Camus examines in much detail the justifiable limits of revolt against the absurd, both vertical and horizontal. This will be the subject of a later chapter. Before moving on to that, however, our present examination should be concluded. The concept of the absurd expresses the impression produced by a state or condition but it does not encompass the causes which produce that condition. These causes, which result in the absurd, particularly in the horizontal, will be the subject of the next two chapters.

5

Man's Malady

T *he Plague* is a work which can be read at three levels. First, it is an excellent novel concerning an imaginary scourge of the bubonic plague at Oran in North Africa. The impression left on the reader is one of increased warmth towards mankind and confidence in his resilience and hidden fortitude which emerge in a time of deep trial. Beneath this level can be seen a portrayal of the life in France during the last war under the German occupation. Madame Jacqueline Bernard, who worked with Camus in the production of the resistance newspaper *Combat,* has pointed out that there are even evidences of parallels with Camus's personal experience. For instance, Dr. Rieux is separated from his wife by the Plague, she suffering from tuberculosis. In Camus's case it was he who had the tuberculosis, and the German occupation kept him in France and his wife in North Africa.

Mme Bernard recounts one amusing little incident which also clearly has its reflection in *The Plague.* She and Camus were working together in the distribution of the paper. Forced to operate clandestinely, their procedure was to make up parcels of copies of the newspapers which they despatched through the mail to fellow-workers who, in turn, distributed them around. One day an error was made in the address to which a parcel was sent, the addressee not being a part of the resistance movement, though he was probably not actively pro-German. Alarmed at having this compro-

mising package delivered to his door, this individual, acting most unwisely, went to the police and reported the matter, protesting his innocence. His story appeared unrealistic and suspect—he was arrested. On hearing this, Camus evidently laughed and made the observation that it was as dangerous to have nothing to do with the resistance movement as to participate in it! This theme appears in *The Plague.* After a certain juncture in Oran, involvement was no longer a matter of personal option. The gates were closed and ". . . the plague became everyone's business."

The third level, and this is the one which primarily occupies us here, is the disease of the plague used as a symbol of the spiritual malady or sickness which is the common lot of all men. It is given to Jean Tarrou, in the very heart of the book, to expound to Dr. Rieux his understanding of this:

"I have realised that we all have the Plague and I have lost my peace. And today I am still trying to find it; still trying to understand those others and not be the mortal enemy of anyone. I only know that one must do what one can to cease being plague-stricken, and that's the only way in which we can hope for some peace or, failing that, a decent death. This, and only this, can bring relief to men and, if not save them, at least do them as little harm as possible and even, sometimes, a little good. So that is why I resolved to have no truck with anything which, directly or indirectly, for good reasons or for bad, brings death to anyone or justifies killing.

"That is why this epidemic has taught me nothing new, except that I must fight it at your side. I know positively (yes, Rieux, I know all there is to know about life—you can see that quite clearly) that each of us has the Plague within him; no one, no one on earth is free from it. And I know, too, that we must keep endless watch on ourselves lest, in a careless moment, we breathe in somebody's face and fasten the infection on him. What's natural is the microbe. All the rest—health, integrity, purity, if you so desire—is the product of the human will, of a vigilance that must never falter. The good man, the man who infects hardly anyone, is the man who has the fewest lapses of attention. And it needs tremendous will power, a never ending tension of the mind, to avoid such lapses. Yes, Rieux, it's a wearying business being plague-stricken. But it is still more wearying to refuse to be it. That's why everybody in the world today looks so tired; everyone is more or

less sick of the Plague. But that is also why some of us, those who want to get the plague out of their systems, feel such a desperate weariness, a weariness from which nothing remains to set us free except death.

"Pending that release, I know I have no place in the world today; once I'd definitely refused to kill, I doomed myself to an exile that can never end. All I maintain is that on this earth there are pestilences. and there are victims, and it's up to us so far as possible, not to join forces with the pestilences. That may sound simple to the point of childishness, but I know it's true. You see, I'd heard such quantities of arguments, which very nearly turned my head, and turned other people's heads enough to make them approve of murder; and I'd come to realise that all our troubles stem from our failure to use plain, clean-cut language. So I resolved to speak, and to act, always quite clearly as this was the only way of setting myself on the right track. That's why I say there are pestilences and there are victims; no more than that. . . . I grant that we should add a third category; that of the true healers. But it's a fact that one doesn't come across many of them, and anyhow it must be a hard vocation. That's why I decided to take, in every predicament, the victim's side, so as to reduce the damage done. Among them I can at least try to discover how one attains to the third category; in other words, to peace." (CT, 1423)

Dr. Rieux asked Tarrou if he had any idea of the path to follow for attaining peace. "Yes," he replied, "the path of sympathy. . . . It comes to this, what interests me is learning how to become a saint."

"But you don't believe in God," says the Doctor.

"Exactly! Can one be a saint without God? That's the problem; in fact, the only problem I'm up against today."

Before making any comment, it is most appropriate to quote a passage from one of the apostle Paul's letters (Romans Ch 7). The comparison between the inward malady, the spiritual plague, which Tarrou finds within himself and against which he constantly strives, and the inward principle that Paul calls 'sin' is quite striking. They are surely talking of the same thing. This quotation also is taken from the translation by J. B. Phillips.

"My own behavior baffles me. For I find myself not doing what I really want to do but doing what I really loathe. Yet surely if I

do things that I really don't want to do it cannot be said that "I" am doing them at all—it must be sin that has made its home in my nature. (And indeed, I know from experience that the carnal side of my being can scarcely be called the home of good!) I often find that I have the will to do good, but not the power. That is, I don't accomplish the good I set out to do, and the evil I don't really want to do I find I am always doing. Yet if I do things that I really don't want to do, it is not, I repeat, "I" who do them, but the sin which has made its home within me. When I come up against the Law I want to do good but in practice I do evil. My conscious mind wholeheartedly endorses the Law, yet I observe an entirely different principle at work in my nature. This is in continual conflict with my conscious attitude, and makes me an unwilling prisoner to the law of sin and death. It is an agonizing situation, and who on earth can set me free from the clutches of my own sinful nature? I thank God there is a way out through Jesus Christ Our Lord."

Camus and Paul are not in agreement as to the remedy but it seems they are talking of exactly the same malady! For Tarrou there is no remedy; it will be a struggle until he is delivered by death. Camus had sought a remedy, or rather to change his nature, as he describes in an important quotation mentioned in a former chapter but which should be repeated here. "As has everyone else, so have I tried. . to correct my nature by applied morality. It is this, alas, which has proved to be the most costly thing for me. With a good deal of effort, and I have made such, one can sometimes manage to conduct oneself according to the dictates of morality, but never to be it." (CE, 11)

Benjamin Franklin knew all about the malady and tried to change himself too. Whenever he noticed an undesirable trait in his character or behavior he set himself a certain period of time to overcome that thing and change it. He kept a calendar on which he noted the dates by which the changes ought to be accomplished. At the end of his life he testified, as did Camus, that through self-discipline he had managed to change the exterior to quite an extent; but that he had never succeeded in effecting one iota of change in his nature or heart.

A young African attended a conference of Christians in the U.S.A. at which he was exhorted by a speaker to put to death his old

nature and be inwardly transformed. His comments afterwards were quite quaint but showed that he had tried harder than the speaker to do what the latter had encouraged him to attempt: "I tried to put my old man to death," he said, "but he nearly killed me! I tried to get on top of him and master him or, to put it differently, to suppress myself; but I couldn't tell who was on top—myself or I!"

We are now in a position to see far more clearly the distinction between that which is absurd and that which is not. A man or group of men who admit the existence of the inward malady, because they have recognized it by experience, and also admit their impotence to change it; that man or group is real. On the other hand anyone who refuses to admit the malady's existence or who preaches morality, the conforming of the exterior to a code of morals, is Pharisaic and absurd.

To Camus, the vast majority of so-called Christians fall into the second category. "Take our moral philosophers, for instance," says Clamence in *The Fall*, "so serious, loving their neighbor and all the rest—nothing distinguishes them from Christians except that they don't preach in Churches." (CF, 133) Earlier in the same book Clamence says: "Believe me, religions are on the wrong track the moment they moralize and fulminate the commandments." (CF, 110)

Will Herberg, in his vitally significant book, *Protestant, Catholic, Jew,* says that there is little difference any longer between the three; having lost their individual vision they have little or nothing left but morality and, of course, in this they are perfectly agreed. What he is saying is that religious institutions in the West are almost all absurd in their busily whitening the outside of the sepulchre with a liberal dose of morality preaching whilst turning a blind eye to the real state of affairs on the inside which is "full of hypocrisy and iniquity." (*Matthew*, 23.28) The absurd man who prefers to maintain the status quo may seem a paragon of virtue and a pillar of society, but he is spiritually dead: The real man may have troubles and be ostracized by the absurd; but he is spiritually alive.

It is almost incredible that Christianity should have strayed so far. It is specifically stated that the Law "keeps slipping into the picture expressly to point out the vast extent of sin"—to shine a light on the malady. (*Romans*, 5.20) It was supposed to be a

" 'Tutor' [which, having proved to us our utter inability to fulfill its demands,] would bring us to Christ." (*Galatians*, 3.24) But men have made it an end in itself and worship it as a kind of ultimate. Of course, for the absurd man who likes his absurdity there is a temporary sense of well-being and self-justification in speaking about being good and doing good. He has satisfaction in a vague sense of some duty fulfilled in sitting weekly for about an hour whilst another tells him he should be good. "Nice society," says Sartre, "believes in God in order to avoid talking about him." (SW, 80) How reluctant the city officials at Oran were at the outset of the Plague to face the facts and their significance; nobody dared mention the word 'Plague'. They tried to pretend to themselves and to others, until the very last minute, that it was something else. Finally, when they could keep up the pretense no longer, they tried to cover up the magnitude of the malady by reporting the deaths in such a way as to make them seem less numerous. "For the plague-stricken their peace of mind is more important than a human life," says Tarrou. "Decent folks must be allowed to sleep easy at night, mustn't they?" he adds with biting sarcasm! (CT, 1422)

It is on the basis of this morality that Meursault is judged, and not on his act. He didn't weep at his mother's funeral, he smoked a cigarette and drank café au lait sitting beside her coffin, he didn't know her exact age, he didn't make provision for her himself but had her put away in the home for old people; the day after the funeral he met Marie and went with her to a comic film etc. etc. The great religions are the chief heralds of this morality, the legal profession—the technical advisers concerning it, and the police—those who enforce it. It was something of a crisis in the life of Clamence, the Lawyer of *The Fall*, when it dawned upon him that he was frequently of less intrinsic worth than those, supposedly guilty of heinous crimes, whom he defended. He tried to shake out of their lethargy a group of young lawyers, whom he had been invited to address, by seeking to explain to them this understanding.

"Let us suppose that I have accepted the defense of some touching citizen, a murderer through jealousy. 'Gentlemen of the jury, consider,' I should say, 'how venial it is to get angry when one sees one's natural goodness put to the test by the malignity of the fair sex. Is it not more serious, on the contrary, to be by chance on this side of the bar, on my own bench, without ever having been good or

having suffered from being duped? I am free, shielded from your severities, yet who am I? A Louis XIV in pride, a billy-goat for lust, a Pharoah for wrath, a king of laziness. I haven't killed anyone? Not yet, to be sure! But have I not let deserving creatures die? Maybe! And maybe I am ready to do so again. Whereas this man —just look at him—will not do so again. He is still absolutely astonished that he could have done what he has.' This speech rather upset my young colleagues. After a moment, they made up their mind to laugh at it—they became completely reassured when, drawing to my conclusion, I invoked the human individual and his supposed rights. That day habit won out." (CF, 94)

With the final words of his address, Clamence falls into the usual platitudes about morality. He had habitually used these for years —after all, it is what the absurd expects—and he did it automatically, without thinking, but not without regret, on this occasion. This slip let the status quo return, giving the ill-at-ease young lawyers the opportunity quickly to brush aside the embarrassing confrontation they had just had with reality.

May we not then say that it is man's malady, hiding behind a mask of morality, that is largely responsible for the creation of the absurd in society, the horizontal, and almost entirely so for its maintenance and support?

This chapter would be incomplete without it being noted that the Scriptures affirm that the Absurd vertically is also a direct consequence of this malady. "And unto Adam He said: Because thou hast hearkened unto the voice of thy wife, and hast eaten of the tree, of which I commanded thee saying, Thou shalt not eat of it: cursed is the ground for thy sake; in toil shalt thou eat of it all the days of thy life; thorns and thistles shall it bring forth to thee; and thou shalt eat the herb of the field; in the sweat of thy face shalt thou eat bread, till thou return unto the ground; for out of it wast thou taken: For dust thou art and unto dust shalt thou return." (*Genesis,* 3.17-9) The cycle is complete and we find ourselves back again where we began with Sisyphus and Solomon.

6

The Root of the Malady

On first reading, *The Fall* (La Chute) appears to be a study of the guilt complex which awakens in a successful young Paris lawyer after an experience on a bridge one night when he makes no effort to rescue a young woman from committing suicide. Indeed, one might imagine that if *The Plague* deals primarily with man's malady, what the apostle Paul calls sin, then *The Fall* deals with acts which the malady provokes man to do, what Paul calls sins, and the sense of guilt which follows such doing.

But this neither takes into account the title, which is clearly an allusion to the biblical Fall, nor the central figure, Jean-Baptiste Clamence (John the Baptist Clemency) who obviously draws his name, if not much of his character, from his biblical namesake. From the latter we may deduce that Camus is heralding some new "way" here.

Clamence brushes aside what he regards as being the Christian's superficial evasion of the issue: "People naturally tried to get some help from His (Jesus Christ's) death. After all, it was a stroke of genius to tell us 'You're not a very pretty sight, that's certain! Well, we won't go into the details, we'll just liquidate it all at once on the cross!' " (CF, 114) He then proceeds to develop and expound his own solution which, whilst helping considerably, he nevertheless has to admit is not the ideal.

As to the title, it would seem to indicate that Camus purposes to wrestle here with the ageless problem of the origin of evil and that he is inviting consideration at least of the biblical Fall. Early in the book Clamence says to his interlocutor: "You are what I call a Sadducee then. If you don't have a knowledge of the Scriptures I admit that won't help you much. That does help you? You do know the Scriptures then? Decidedly you interest me." (CE, 1478) If we are fully to understand what Camus intends to imply by his title to this work it will be against the background of a comprehension of its scriptural significance.

There are two falls mentioned in the Bible, the Fall of Satan and the Fall of Adam. Jesus Christ said he witnessed the first: "I beheld Satan fallen like lightning from heaven." (*Luke*, 10.18) This forced expulsion was occasioned by an inward change in this being which made him unfit to continue any longer in his former lofty habitat and high calling. "Thou wast the anointed Cherub that covereth: and I set thee so that thou wast upon the holy mountain of God. . . . Thou wast perfect in thy ways from the day that thou wast created, till unrighteousness (twistedness) was found in thee. . . . Thine heart was lifted up because of thy beauty, thou hast corrupted thy wisdom by reason of thy brightness: I have cast thee to the ground." (*Ezekiel*, 28.14-7) This moment could be called the birth of self-consciousness. Given freedom of will to choose, this being evidently contemplated himself and that self-consciousness produced pride, the desire to be above others and to be recognized as such. Once loosed, pride knows no bounds and we soon find this fallen creature obsessed by it: "I will ascend into heaven, I will exalt my throne above the stars of God: and I will sit upon the mount of congregation, in the uttermost parts of the north: I will ascend above the heights of the clouds; I will be like the Most High." (Isaiah, 14.13-4) Without doubt this has some bearing upon our subject here for Clamence echoes this obsession: "I lived consequently without any other continuity than that, from day to day, of I, I, I." (CF,50)

The Fall of Adam, on the other hand, was a Fall from innocence as a result of disobedience. He was told to eat of the tree of life and not to touch the tree of the knowledge of good and evil; but he was tempted and fell. The result of his fall, however, was to awaken a guilty conscience in him which manifested itself first in his

hiding from God and seeking to cover his shame and then, when faced with what he had done, in his trying to make excuses for himself.

Clamence's fall cannot be wholly identified with either of these and yet we can see traces of both in it. He shares with Satan the intense desire to be above others, even God; and with Adam the feeling that somehow he has to excuse and justify that which he knows is despicable about himself. Satan and Adam fall from innocence, but not so Clamence. He falls simply because he discovers his true nature. He had thought he was a veritable paragon of virtue, a man who was perfect in all his ways. Through one crisis after another, he discovers little by little the motives which lie back of his actions; and the discovery undoes him and drains him of the power to continue playing the role of the charming, self-sacrificial philanthropic lawyer and pillar of society he had thought himself to be. To his amazement and horror he finds out that every action, thought, and motive has behind it a hidden force of pride. Pride being that stubborn indomitable desire and unquenchable thirst to be above everyone if possible but, if that cannot be, at least above someone! I know of no book in which this aspect of the human heart is disclosed more ruthlessly and piercingly.

"I was always in harmony," says Clamence, speaking of the years which preceded this spiritual awakening, "hence my popularity was great and my successes in society innumerable. I was acceptable in appearance; I revealed myself to be both a tireless dancer and an unobtrusively learned man; I managed to love simultaneously —and this is not easy—women and justice; I indulged in sports and the fine arts—in short, I'll not go on for fear you might suspect self-flattery. But just imagine, I beg you, a man at the height of his powers, in perfect health, generously gifted, skilled in bodily exercises as in those of the mind, neither rich nor poor, sleeping well, and fundamentally pleased with himself without showing this otherwise than by a felicitous sociability. You will readily see how I can speak, without immodesty, of a successful life. . . . This harmony in me, the relaxed mastery in me that other people felt, even to telling me sometimes that it helped them in life. Hence my company was in demand. . . . To tell the truth, just from being so fully and simply a man, I looked upon myself as being something

of a superman. I was of respectable but humble birth (my father was an officer), and yet, certain mornings, let me confess it humbly, I felt like a king's son, or a burning bush. . . . As a result of being showered with blessings, I felt (I hesitate to admit it) marked out. Personally marked out, among all for that long and uninterrupted success. . . . When I add that I had no religion you can see even better how extraordinary that conviction was. Whether ordinary or not, it served for some time to raise me above the daily routine and I literally soared for a period of years, for which, to tell the truth, I still long in my heart of hearts." (CF, 27) Clamence was a young bachelor. What a perfect description of the mental attitude of a spiritually unaware young man who imagines himself secure in his intellectual endowment and physical fitness and who, unanchored by marriage, is sublimely confident that there is nothing in heaven or on earth which could resist his success. It is from this state of ignorance, rather than innocence, that he falls!

The fall begins for him deep inside his heart and gradually extends outward to encompass his relationships with others until he and the world he lives in are all in it together. It is clearly not without design that Camus chose a dingy backstreet of Amsterdam famed for its canals, fogs, rain, and grey sea as the habitat of Clamence after the discovery of the true nature of himself; and Paris with all its glitter, animation, and excitement as the setting for his 'innocent' youth. Truly, ignorance is bliss!

What was the experience which precipitated the change, which punctured the illusion and began the fall of Clamence? Let him tell it in his own words: "I soared until the evening when. . . . But no, that's another matter and it must be forgotten. Anyway, I am perhaps exaggerating. I was at ease in everything, to be sure, but at the same time satisfied with nothing. Each joy made me desire another. I went from festivity to festivity. . . . I ran on like that, always heaped with favors, never satiated, without knowing where to stop, until the day—until the evening rather when the music stopped and the lights went out. The gay party at which I had been so happy." (CF, 30)

How beautifully this describes the 'innocent' state; boundless energy and enthusiasm, and only one little factor, fly in the ointment, which quietly but persistently questions the condition—"at

ease in everything . . . but satisfied with nothing." Whenever this little ogre of inability to achieve full satisfaction reared its head he would "rush forth anew" in the vain hope that at the next party, around the next corner would be someone or something which would fully satisfy.

As to women, he was a veritable Don Juan. No sooner had he conquered one than his appetite for her abated and the huntsman in him awoke all over again, driving him to cast about further afield. As he moved on, however, it was without relinquishing from his side any of his former conquests; his possessiveness would not let him countenance the thought of any he had won being stolen from him. A thirst for something new coupled with a dogged determination to keep what he had already gained—always running but never arriving.

"Until the evening when. . ." How reticent Clamence is to speak of this experience. He keeps on putting it off and it is not until halfway through the book that he finally opens up and tells about it. We have to know a person very well before we will recount to him any personal solitary experience in which our pride received a blow. We shall be quick to tell of those incidents which took place in public, which someone else saw; in fact we shall probably look for occasions to recount such, giving our interpretation so as to forestall what others might say and take the sting out of their remarks in advance! But when some experience comes our way which no one knows anything about and in which we are made to see the ugliness of our pride—we shall not readily recount that to others. There are probably very few persons who, at one time or another, have not had such an experience which they never recounted to another soul. Garcin, the hero of *No Exit* by Sartre, had discovered he was a coward and, appalled by his discovery, tried to pretend to himself that it was not so. He had behaved like a brute and mistreated his wife abominably but it didn't worry him in the least that others should know these things because they did not touch his pride. What he couldn't bear was the thought that others might think him to be a coward—that would be a mortal blow from which his pride could never recover! Hence he made every effort at first to avoid engaging in conversation with Estelle and Inez lest they should unearth his secret. After inadvertently letting the cat out of the bag, and how difficult this is to avoid as it is constantly preying on the

mind, he spends the rest of the play making excuses, trying to justify himself and regain a position of respect in their eyes.

What happened on the evening when "the music stopped and the lights went out"? We will let Clamence tell his own story. "That particular night in November, I was returning to the left bank and my home by way of the Pont Royal. It was an hour past midnight, a fine rain was falling, a drizzle rather, that scattered the few people on the streets. I had just left a mistress who was surely asleep. I was enjoying that walk, a little numbed, my body calmed and irrigated by a flow of blood gentle as the falling rain. On the bridge I passed behind a figure leaning over the railing and seeming to stare at the river. On a closer view, I made out a slim woman dressed in black. The back of her neck, cool and damp between her dark hair and coat collar, stirred me. But I went on after a moment's hesitation. At the end of the bridge I followed the quays towards Saint-Michel, where I lived. I had already gone some fifty yards when I heard the sound—which, despite the distance, seemed dreadfully loud in the midnight silence—of a body striking water. I stopped short, but without turning around. Almost at once I heard a cry, repeated several times, which was going downstream; then it suddenly ceased. The silence that followed, as the night suddenly stood still, seemed interminable. I wanted to run and yet did not stir. I was trembling, I believe from cold and shock. I told myself that I had to be quick and I felt an irresistible weakness steal over me. I have forgotten what I thought then. "Too late, too far . . ." or something like that. I was still listening as I stood motionless. Then, slowly, under the rain, I went away. I informed no one. . . . The next day and the days following I didn't read the papers." (CF, 69)

Why did he not run back, dive in the river, and save the girl? It was the middle of the night, no one was around, and thus Clamence acted directly out of his nature uncurbed by the influence that would have been exerted upon him by the presence of an audience. Had it happened in the daytime he would doubtless have leapt into the river and been acclaimed a public hero.

On another occasion, having escorted a blind person across the street, he noticed that quite unconsciously he had raised his hat before moving on. It dawned upon him that this could not have been for the benefit of the blind man, for he could not see; it had

been for those who were standing by and watching—his audience. He was playing a role and the role governed his actions. On this occasion, however, the stage was darkened and there was no audience, so the role fell from him and his nature in its nakedness reacted. Not a soul knew he was there, his public image would be untouched by his doing nothing. If he jumped in and tried to save the woman and succeeded, his presence and involvement in such a situation at that hour of the night might have raised questions; if he failed he might well lose his own life in the attempt. Better to keep right out of it!

But he did not arrive at his conclusion as easily as that. There was a conflict which revealed within him, just as it had to Tarrou as described in the preceding chapter, the presence of two natures which were inimical to one another. He wanted to do the right thing but another force in him won out and he did what he despised. "I wanted to run and yet did not stir. . . . I told myself I had to be quick and I felt an irresistible weakness steal over me." Had there been an audience to activate his pride, then pride plus his better self would have overcome and put on the show he desired and it would have been: "I wanted to run and ran. . . . I told myself I had to be quick and I dropped all else and dashed to her rescue!" There was no audience, pride was dormant, and he discovered that this other side of him, which he hated, was too strong for him and, what was worse, that its nature was that of a coward.

Up to this point in his life, weakness and failure were two words which had no place in the vocabulary of Clamence. This experience, however, marks a turning point, an awakening to this other nature which hitherto he had not known existed; and he can never be the same again. He carries on, however, as if nothing out of the ordinary had transpired. His friends do not notice any difference, but in him a spiritual Achilles tendon has been cut. The next development is some two or three years later; an incident takes place as he is crossing a bridge over the Seine a little upstream from where on that fateful night the girl had leapt into the river.

"I had gone up on the Pont des Arts," says Clamence, "deserted at that hour, to look at the river which could hardly be made out now that night had come. Facing the Vert-Galant, I dominated the island. I felt rising within me a vast feeling of power and—I don't know how to express it—of completion, which cheered my heart.

I straightened up and was about to light a cigarette, a cigarette of satisfaction, when, at that very moment, a laugh burst out behind me. Taken by surprise, I wheeled around; there was no one there. I stepped to the railing; no barge or boat. I turned back toward the island and, again, heard the laughter behind me, a little farther off as if it were going downstream. I stood there motionless. The sound of the laughter was decreasing, but I could still hear it distinctly behind me, come from nowhere unless from the water. At the same time I was aware of the rapid beating of my heart. Please don't misunderstand me; there was nothing mysterious about that laugh; it was a good, hearty, almost friendly laugh, which reestablished the proper proportions. . . . That evening I rang up a friend of mine, who wasn't home. I was hesitating about going out when, suddenly, I heard laughter under my windows. I opened them. On a sidewalk in fact some youths were loudly saying good-night. I shrugged my shoulders as I closed the windows; after all, I had a brief to study. I went into the bathroom to drink a glass of water. My reflection was smiling in the mirror, but it seemed to me that my smile was double." (CF, 38)

There are at least two different sorts of laughter. On the one hand, there is the spontaneous expression of joy occasioned by some release or deliverance: "When the Lord turned against the captivity of Zion, we were like unto them that dream. Then was our mouth filled with laughter, and our tongue with singing." (*Psalm* 126, 1-2) On the other hand, there is a type with an altogether other note—an expression of judgment. It is stated in several places in the Psalms that God laughs and on each occasion the nature of his laughter is the latter type. Someone or ones are vaunting themselves against God or His people and imagine they can get away with it. Prior to his acting in judgment, God laughs at them. "Why do the nations rage, and the people imagine a vain thing? The kings of the earth set themselves and the rulers take counsel together against the Lord and against His anointed, saying, Let us break their bands asunder and cast away their cords from us. He that sitteth in the heavens shall laugh: The Lord shall have them in derision." (*Psalm*, 2, 1-4) Or another example: "The wicked plotteth against the just and gnasheth upon him with his teeth. The Lord shall laugh at him for He seeth that his day is coming." (*Psalm* 37, 12-3)

It is this latter type of laughter that Clamence heard. If the nations and the wicked of these two psalms had heard the laughter of God, they would have had misgivings about the outcome of their course of action. "If this or that happens to such and such a person, I shall really laugh," we say, and thereby indicate that we feel that person richly deserves that end. Our laughter is a form of judgment; we are exulting that justice is being meted out. There are few experiences more unnerving and unsettling to human pride than to suspect that others are laughing at us behind our back, particularly if we have no idea of the cause of the laughter. Clamence had witnessed the girl's suicide, but no one knew that he was there, so he had thought; but now, two years later, there is a laugh behind him. Is someone laughing *at him*? Had someone else witnessed that scene? Did someone else know what he did or rather did not do? This crisis marked the second major step in his fall. That night on the bridge when he let the girl drown he had awakened to another and cowardly nature within him; but at least he was the only one who knew anything about it and he could hide his secret from society. But the laugh changes all that. Was there perchance someone who did know, had there been a hidden witness? He can never again look any man absolutely straight in the face, everyman was suspect, any man could know about him.

Hitherto his friends and acquaintances had been no more than the context for his success and he the center of their adoring worship. Now there was a question, he was no longer sure of himself with them. "The circle of which I was the center broke and they lined up in a row as on a judge's bench. In short, the moment I grasped that there was something to judge in me, I realised that there was in them an irresistible vocation for judgment. Yes, they were there as before, but they were laughing. Or rather it seemed to me that everyone I encountered was looking at me with a hidden smile. I even had the impression at that time that people were tripping me up. Two or three times, in fact, I stumbled as I entered public places. Once, even, I went sprawling on the floor! . . . Once my attention was aroused, it was not hard for me to discover that I had enemies." Indeed, it was not just that he had enemies: "The day I was alerted I became lucid; I received all the wounds at the same time and lost my strength all at once. The whole universe began to laugh at me." (CF, 78)

Generally speaking, there appears to be a conflict between the principles of innocence and guilt in the works of Camus. Meursault is convinced of his innocence whereas, after his fall, Clamence is obsessed by his guilt. Meursault feels innocent of being alive — he chose neither to exist nor the circumstances in which he existed. That is as far as *The Stranger* goes — it does not deal with the *Malady* and its consequences. Clamence felt innocent during his period of blissful ignorance but, once he awoke to the other nature in him and despised it, he felt guilty. In that he despised this other nature, he judged it and thereby unconsciously confessed there was something in him which all others would be justified in judging. This latter condition is the source of guilt feelings.

Unable to bear being laughed at, man tries by all means to deflect the judgment of others from himself. "People hasten to judge others in order not to be judged themselves." (CF, 80) It is rather like the traffic in Paris! He who blows his horn first on entering an intersection has the right of way! He who fires a judging barb first has the advantage over the other who is taken unawares. Yet the respite obtained is short. A longer reprieve can be found in riches because "wealth shields from judgment, takes you out of the subway crowd to enclose you in a chromium-plated automobile, isolates you in huge protected lawns, pullmans, first-class cabins. Wealth, however, is not an acquittal but a reprieve, and that's always worth taking." (CF, 82)

Clamence went even further. When asked to address a group of young lawyers—the incident is also recorded in the preceding chapter—he questioned in his speech whether the lawyers and judges were any more moral at heart than those they were judging. His listeners were at first shocked but quickly resorted to laughter to overcome their embarrassment. He had felt provoked to do this because of the stifling unreality of the atmosphere around him. He hoped that through judging the legal profession, of which he was a part, he would be able to find his release. But the release he found was only temporary, a kind of half-way cure. "You see" he says, "it is not enough to accuse yourself in order to clear yourself; otherwise, I'd be as innocent as a lamb. One must accuse oneself in a certain way which it took me considerable time to perfect. I did not discover it until I fell into the most utterly forlorn state. Until then the laughter continued to drift my way, without my random

efforts succeeding in divesting it of its benevolent, almost tender quality that hurt me." (CF, 95)

He regards the quest for a solution to this problem as being a 'call' which placed him in a position where "I had to answer, or at least seek an answer." Here is the essence of the book. Man's pride makes it insufferable for him to be judged by others and he is driven to find a means by which he can if possible nullify or, failing that, at least parry that judgment. Bondage is when we are trapped and hemmed in by the criticism and judgment of our fellows; freedom is when we can escape from all that, because that is the worst we can encounter. "God is not needed to create guilt or to punish," says Clamence. "Our fellow men suffice, aided by ourselves. You are speaking of the last judgment. Allow me to laugh respectfully. I shall wait for it resolutely, for I have known what is worse, the judgment of men." (CF, 110)

He sought to escape first by finding some woman for whom he might have the 'true love' of which the story books speak. But his problem was that for so many years he had been exclusively in love with himself. He tried living in chastity, but that gave no release. Finally he turned to debauchery, "a substitute for love, which quiets the laughter." (CF, 102) This last means was the most effective: "Tubercular lungs are cured by drying up and gradually asphyxiate their happy owner. So it was with me as, I peacefully died of my cure." (CF, 106)) Thus life continued until the day he took a sea voyage with a woman friend to celebrate his 'cure'. He was on the upper deck of an ocean liner when he perceived a black speck on the steel-gray sea. He turned away at once and his heart began to beat wildly. When he forced himself to look again, the black speck had disappeared. He was on the point of shouting, calling for help, when it reappeared. It was just a piece of flotsam left behind by some ship and he had been silly enough to think it might have been a person drowning! That just showed how far he was from solving his problem and how close at hand was the memory of that fateful night "when the music stopped and the lights went out." "Then," he said, "I realised, calmly as you resign yourself to an idea, the truth of which you have long known, that that cry which had sounded behind me over the Seine years ago had never ceased . . . that it would continue to await me on seas and rivers, every-

where, in short, where lies the bitterwater of my baptism. . . . I realised definitively that I was not cured!" (CF, 108)

It is at the end of the book that Clamence unfolds his method of escaping the judgment and criticism of his fellowmen. "I had to find another means of extending judgment to everybody in order to make it weigh less heavily on my shoulders." (CF, 137) He explains. "My idea is both simple and fertile. How could I get everyone involved in order to have the right to sit calmly on the outside myself? Should I climb up to the pulpit, like many of my illustrious contemporaries, and curse humanity? Very dangerous, that is! One day or one night, laughter bursts out without a warning. The judgment you are passing on others eventually snaps back in your face, causing some damage. And so what? you ask. Well, here's the stroke of genius. . . . Inasmuch as one couldn't condemn others without immediately judging oneself, one has to overwhelm oneself to have the right to judge others. Inasmuch as some day every judge ends up a penitent, one has to travel the road in the opposite direction and practice the profession of penitent to be able to end up a judge." (CF, 137)

He then goes on to explain how he practices this novel function of Judge-Penitent. He starts by accusing himself up hill and down dale and then gradually adapts his accusation to his listener, leading him to go one better. "I mingle what concerns me with what concerns others. I choose the features we have in common . . . the failings we share. With all that I construct a portrait which is the image of all and of no one. A mask, in short, rather like those carnival masks which are both lifelike and stylized, so that they make people say: "Why, surely I've met him!" When the portrait is finished I show it with great sorrow: "This, alas, is what I am!" The prosecutor's charge is finished. But at the same time the portrait which I hold out to my contemporaries becomes a mirror. I start by saying ' I am the lowest of the low,' then, imperceptibly, I pass from the 'I' to the 'We'. When I get to 'this is what we are,' the trick has been played and I can tell them off. I am like them, to be sure; we are in the soup together. However, I have a superiority in that I know it and this gives me the right to speak. . . . The more I accuse myself the more I have the right to judge you." (CF, 139) But what does he gain from this judgment of others? Here lies the key to the whole matter. "I dominate at last . . . but for ever" says

Clamence, "I have found a mountain top to which I alone can climb and from which I can judge everybody." (CF, 142)

This chapter has been lengthy and the progressive development of Clamence's spiritual life somewhat protracted—a synopsis may be helpful to focus the principles which he discovererd. It was in blissful ignorance that he sailed along in his youth with boundless confidence in himself until the fateful night on the bridge when he became aware of the presence of another nature within himself which he despised. At once, in his own conscience, he judges that nature by feeling guilty—for guilt feelings are no more than self-judgment. When he hears a laugh, two or three years later, he becomes conscious that others too have discovered the presence within him of something worthy of being judged. His feeling of wellbeing and ascendancy is quite lost, he is imprisoned and kept under by the constant barrage from his own and others' accusing fingers. He had lost the ability to feel ABOVE and he desperately needed to get it back again in order to breathe freely. He tried successively women, chastity, and debauchery to drown out this frustration and find escape for his soul which longed to "soar" once again. He thought he was succeeding, that the past was buried and forgotten, and that he was 'cured'; but the experience on the ocean liner proved once and for all that he had made no headway whatsoever. Finally he lights upon a solution. If, whenever one mounts a peak, one will ultimately be dethroned either by the inescapable inward voice of the conscience which evokes guilt or by the judgments and criticisms of others, then the only solution is to reverse the process and to abase oneself in the dust and then show to the others that that is where they also are in reality. Then, at last, a position of ascendancy above all others will have been attained in that one is the pioneer of this thing and all others the followers.

Is it a perfect solution? No! Clamence has to admit that "at long intervals, on a really beautiful night, I occasionally hear a distant laugh and again I doubt. But I quickly crush everything, people and things, under the weight of my own infirmity, and at once I perk up." He adds briefly: "To be sure, my solution is not the ideal!" (CF, 142)

The last few lines of the book are heavy with significance "the words which ring in my ears night after night—'Oh young lady!

Throw yourself once more in the water so that I can have a second chance to save both of us.' A second chance, huh, how unwise! Just suppose that you were to be taken at your word? You would have to go ahead with it. Brr..! The water is so cold! But don't let's worry! It's too late, now, it will always be too late. Fortunately!" (CT, 1549)

If he had a second chance and did dive in and save the girl, would he be able to escape back again to that realm of bliss he lived in whilst still ignorant of the other nature within himself? No! It is too late; once the illusion is destroyed there is no recapturing it. But why is he glad that it will always be too late? There is a kind of rest possible when a situation has been accepted and defeat admitted; indeed this gives a kind of superiority as one can laugh at those who are still struggling against impossible odds. At the end of Sartre's *No Exit*, Garcin, the hero, comes to the same position when he sees that he is never going to change Inez's estimate of him, that he is a coward. "Continuons!" he says. "All right!" well let's just go on with life!" (SH, 76) Saint-Exupéry spoke of the same principle: "I thought myself to be lost, I believed I'd plumbed the very depths of despair but, once I'd resigned myself, I experienced peace." (SO, 244)

7

Spiritual Revolt

There is a logical progression which follows directly from the matters dealt with in the last three chapters; namely, the effects of the absurd and man's malady on religious institutions, their protagonists, and the doctrines that the latter devise. This is perhaps a suitable juncture, however, to deviate for a moment and examine the nature of the revolt, as advocated by Camus, against the absurd, both horizontal and vertical, and against the condition of man resulting from his malady.

The chief exponent of this spiritual revolt in the works of Camus is Jean Tarrou of *The Plague*. It is his ambition to be a saint whereas Dr. Rieux aspires to be a 'man'. Tarrou assures the doctor that the latter is more difficult. Without doubt these two characters represent the two sides, spiritual and practical, of Camus's ideal man. Dr. Rieux fights the absurd by pitting all his strength against the physical sufferings of man: "Perhaps it is better for God that we don't believe in him," he says, "and that we fight with all our strength against death without raising our eyes heavenwards where he is silent!" (CT, 1321) Tarrou, on the other hand, is always looking for the significance behind the surface of things; he is meditative. We first make his acquaintance standing in a stairway, quietly smoking a cigarette as he contemplates with great interest a rat expiring from the bubonic plague. We see him for the last time as he himself dies of the plague in Dr. Rieux's apartment,

59

concerned that if he has to die he shall do so worthily and "make a good end of it." (CT, 1451) He had sought to arrive at peace by the way of sympathy, and Dr. Rieux wonders whether he attained his goal.

To understand Tarrou's revolt we must go back to his beginnings and see what set him going down this path. Like Clamence of *The Fall*, he had a period of ignorance concerning the true state of man which he interpreted as innocence. This period was abruptly terminated the day he awoke and began to think seriously. We will let him recount the incident which precipitated this change.

"My father had one peculiarity. The big railway directory was his bedside book. Not that he often took a train, almost his only journeys were to Brittany where he had a small country house to which he went every summer. But he was a walking timetable. He could tell you the exact times of departure and arrival of the Paris-Berlin express, how to get from Lyon to Warsaw, which trains to take and at what hours, the precise distance between any two capital cities you might mention. Could you tell me off-hand how to get from Briancon to Chamonix? Even the station-master would scratch his head! Well, my father had the answer pat. Almost every evening he enlarged his knowledge of the subject and he prided himself on it. This hobby of his much amused me. I would put complicated travel problems to him and check his answers later in the directory. They were invariably correct. My father and I got on excellently, thanks largely to these railway games we played in the evenings. I was exactly the audience he needed, attentive and appreciative. Personally, I regarded this accomplishment of his as quite as admirable in its way as most accomplishments. But I'm letting my tongue run away with me, and attributing too much importance to that worthy man. Actually he played only an indirect role in the great change of heart about which I want to tell you.

"When I was seventeen, my father asked me to come and hear him speak in court. There was a big case on at the assizes and probably he thought I'd see him to his best advantage. Also, I suspect he hoped I'd be duly impressed by the pomp and ceremony of the law and encouraged to take up his profession. I could tell he was keen on my going, and the prospect of seeing a side of my father's character so different from that we saw at home appealed to me. Those were absolutely the only reasons I had for going to the trial.

What happened in a court had always seemed to me as natural, as much in the order of things as a military parade on the Fourteenth of July, or a school commencement. My notions on the subject were purely abstract, and I'd never given it serious thought. The only picture I carried away with me of that day's proceedings was a picture of the criminal. I have no doubt that he was guilty, of what crime is no great matter. That little man of about thirty with sparse, sandy hair seemed so eager to confess everything, so genuinely horrified by what he had done, and after a few minutes I had eyes for nothing and nobody else. He looked like a yellow owl scared by too much light. His tie was slightly awry. He kept biting his nails, those of one hand, only his right. I needn't go on, need I? He was a living human being. As for me, it came on me suddenly in a flash of understanding, until then I had thought of him only under his commonplace official designation as the defendant, and though I can't quite say I forgot my father, something seemed to grip my vitals at that moment and riveted all my attention on the little man in the dock. I hardly heard what was being said. I only knew that they were set on killing that living man, and an uprush of some elemental instinct like a wave had swept me to his side, and I did not really wake up until my father rose to address the court. In his red garment, he was another man. No longer congenial or good-natured, his mouth spewed out long turgid phrases like an endless stream of snakes. I realised that he was clamoring for the prisoner's death, telling the jury they owed it to society to find him guilty. He went so far as to demand that the man should have his head cut off. Not exactly in those words, I admit; he must pay the supreme penalty was the formula. But the difference really was slight, and the result was the same. He had the head he asked for, only of course it wasn't he who did the actual job. I, who saw the whole business to its conclusion, felt a far closer, more terrifying intimacy with that wretched man than my father could ever have felt. Nevertheless, it fell to him in the course of his duties to be present at what is politely termed the prisoner's last moments. From that day on, I couldn't even see the railway directory without a shudder of disgust. I took a horrified interest in legal proceedings, death sentences, executions, and I realised with dismay that my father must often have witnessed those brutal murders. Probably you're expecting me to tell you that I left home at once. No, I stayed

for many months, nearly a year in fact. Then, one evening my father asked for the alarm clock as he had to get up early. I couldn't sleep that night. Next day, when he came home I'd gone." (CT, 1418)

It was the vital humanity of the defendant, the scared yellow owl, on the one hand, and the ruthless inhumanity of his father in the exercise of his profession, on the other, that shocked Tarrou into a new consciousness. His father had seemingly switched off all emotion and sympathy on entering the court and become like the railroad time-table, a book full of inanimate specifications which governed the behavior of an entire system. Application of the law took over the man and he became the relentless exponent of it. As he thought of this experience, Tarrou came finally to the conclusion that the society in which he lived was founded upon the death sentence. Having lost his peace on discovering that all men in some measure participate in this meteing out of condemnation, he resolved that for his part from that moment onwards he "would have no truck with anything which, directly or indirectly, for good reasons or bad, brings death to anyone or justifies others' putting anyone to death" (CT, 1423)

This resolution was not easy for him to carry out, however, for he discovered in himself a penchant towards judgment. He found out that neither he nor anyone else was free from the sickness of the plague and that "we must keep endless watch on ourselves lest in a careless moment we breathe in somebody's face and fasten the infection on him." He aspired to be "the good man" who, he said, is "the man who hardly infects anyone — the man who has the fewest lapses of attention." Whilst treading this path of personal sanctification he sought also not to arouse the enmity of others: "today I am still trying to find my peace and not be the mortal enemy of anyone." (CT, 1423) As to others, he decided "in every predicament to take the victim's side so as to reduce the damage done." (CT, 1424)

Earlier in the book Dr Rieux had said to Tarrou that "the order of the world is governed by death." (CT, 1321) His revolt was against physical death in his patients whereas Tarrou's was first against himself spiritually as he sought to reduce to a minimum the occasions on which the plague infected others through his lips and secondly against the fruit of judgment and condemnation by taking the part of the condemned so as to ease their burden. It is significant

that he befriends and tries to help such a one as Cottard, perhaps the most unsavory character of *The Plague,* whom everyone else, except Dr. Rieux and Grand, suspected and seemed to avoid. Cottard had evidently committed some crime serious enough to make him attempt suicide and for which the police sought to take him into custody after the plague was over; but none of this in the least deterred Tarrou.

There is a persistent note of sadness, almost of tragedy, about the quest of Tarrou. "I know I have no place in the world today" he says. "Once I'd definitely refused to kill, I doomed myself to an exile that can never end. I leave it to others to make history." (CT, 1424) He had no hope of fully attaining his goal; the best he could look for would be a partial fulfilment and that would be by dint of constant struggle. "Yes Rieux, it's a wearying business, being plague-stricken. But it's still more wearying to refuse to be it. That's why everybody in the world looks so tired, everyone is more or less sick of the plague. But that is also why some of us, those who want to get the plague out of their systems, feel such a desperate weariness, a weariness from which nothing remains to set us free except death." (CT, 1424)

That physical life should be terminated by death is inevitable, a fact which man cannot alter; but Dr Rieux could postpone and mollify this certainty by medicine — he could extend life. The death sentence, applied by man in society as the instrument of justice, however, was most unsatisfactory both in its lacking a foundation of moral clarity and fairness and there being nothing one could do to change it as Meursault realised when he considered the verdict which had been pronounced upon him. "For really, when one came to think of it, there was a disproportion between the judgment on which it was based and the unalterable sequence of events starting from the moment when that judgment was delivered. The fact that the verdict was read out at eight p.m., rather than five, the fact that it might have been quite different, that it was given by men who change their underclothes, and was credited to so vague an entity as the 'French People' — for that matter, why not to the Chinese or German people? All of these facts seemed to deprive the court's decision of much of its gravity. Yet I could but recognize that, from the moment the verdict was given, its effects became as cogent, as tangible, as, for example, this wall against which I was lying, press-

ing my back to it." (CS, 137) No wonder that, early in *The Fall,*
Clamence makes the observation: "It can't be denied that, for the
moment at least, we have to have judges, don't we? However, I
could not understand how a man could offer himself to perform
such a surprising function. I accepted the fact because I saw it, but
rather as I accepted locusts!" (CF, 18)

Unhappily it is not just society as a whole that is governed legally
by the principle of judgment and just retribution; religious institutions have fallen into the same pattern. It is in the last of the short
stories of *The Exile and the Kingdom—The Stone which Grows—*
that this is brought to light most clearly. D'Arrast, a French con-
struction engineer, travels to Iguape, a remote town in Brazil, where
he is to build a dam which will help prevent flooding in the poorer
native section of town during the rainy season. His first encounter
with the absurd imported French society is packed with judgment.
He is accosted by the chief of police who is drunk and demands to
see his passport which he asserts is not in order. The town judge is
close by and intervenes, dismissing the chief of police summarily
and apologizing for him to D'Arrast. The judge and other town
officials then convene to discuss what would be a suitable punishment for the chief of police for his disgraceful behavior; finally
they ask D'Arrast to make the decision and choose the penalty
which he feels would be just. It is with the greatest difficulty that
he manages to persuade them that the incident was without real
importance, that he did not feel irked or insulted by the chief of
police and that he would much rather that no punishment was
given; they finally acquiesce. An excellent case of Tarrou's philosophy — no judgment came out of his own mouth and he took
the side of the defendant without rousing the animosity of his
accusers. Having survived this test, he is now to encounter something far stronger and more subtle with deep superstitious roots,
namely judgment in religious institutions.

After this brief skirmish with the absurd in society, D'Arrast goes
down to the native section of the town by the river to meet the
people and assess the magnitude of the task ahead of him. Here he
meets Le Coq (The Cook) and a friendship strikes up at once between the two. D'Arrast soon learns that Le Coq is to participate
in a religious procession the following day; he has a debt to pay.
"I was at sea off Iguape in a little tanker which carried provisions

to the ports up and down the coast. Fire broke out . . . . we managed to get the boats into the water . . . . During the night, the sea got up, the boat rolled and I fell overboard. When I came to the surface I hit my head on the underside of the boat. I drifted. The night was pitch black, the seas were high and I swim poorly; and I was afraid. Suddenly I saw a light in the distance and recognized the dome of the church of the Good Jesus at Iguape. Then I said to the Good Jesus that I would carry a stone weighing fifty kilos on my head during the procession if he would save me. You will never believe me but the seas became calm and my heart too! I swam steadily, I was happy, and I arrived at the shore. Tomorrow I will keep my promise." (CT, 1668)

Le Coq has a problem, however. On the night preceding the procession there are traditional festivities which he hates to miss. There is alcohol, smoking, and primitive hypnotic dancing. He begs D'Arrast to promise to force him to go to bed early so that he will be strong enough to fulfil his promise the following day. When the festivities are well under way, however, Le Coq becomes captivated by the atmosphere and refuses all D'Arrast's efforts to drag him away. The next day, of course, he is in no condition to fulfil his promise. Nevertheless, he starts off and, with a colossal effort, manages to keep going until he is almost in sight of the church which marks the end of the procession and into which he should carry the stone. Finally he falls, gets up again, and continues a little "with a kind of jerky trot, not like someone who is trying to make forward progress but as if he was trying to escape from the load which was crushing him, as if he was trying to lighten it by his movement. D'Arrast found himself, without knowing how he got to be there, on his right side." (CT, 1681) Despite all his efforts to encourage the little man, he weakens, and it is obvious that there is not the power in him to continue much longer. "He took as deep a breath as he could and stopped dead. He tottered again, staggered three steps, wobbled. Suddenly the stone slipped onto his shoulder, making a gash in it, and then to the ground and Le Coq, off balance, flopped over by the side of it. Those who were leading his way and encouraging him rushed back shouting; one of them took hold of the pad of ivy (which served as a cushion for his head) while the others took up the stone in order to load Le Coq with it again.

D'Arrast, leaning over him, wiped the blood and dust from his

shoulder with his hand whilst the little man panted, his face pressed
to the ground. He heard nothing and lay there motionless. His
mouth opened wide each time he drew a breath as if it were his
last. D'Arrast put his arm around him and lifted him up as easily
as if he had been a child.... Enormous tears silently flooded his
agonized face. He wanted to speak, he was speaking but his mouth
could hardly form the words. "I promised!" he was saying, and then
"Oh Captain, Oh Captain!" and the tears drowned his voice....
D'Arrast looked at him without knowing what to say. He, D'Arrast,
turned towards the crowd which was crying out again in the distance. Suddenly, he snatched the pad of ivy from the hands of the
one who was carrying it and strode towards the stone. He motioned
to those standing by to lift it up and he put it on his head almost
without effort.... He entered the public square amidst the din of
bells and exploding firecrackers and made his way between two
lines of spectators, who looked at him with astonishment but now
in complete silence. He advanced with the same determined step
and the crowd opened up a way for him to the church. Despite the
weight which was beginning to bear down on his head and neck he
saw the church and the portable shrine which seemed to be waiting
for him in the outer court. He walked directly towards it and had
already passed the center of the square when violently, without
knowing why, he veered off to the left and turned away from the
direction of the church, obliging the pilgrims to face him." (CT,
1681) He then carries the stone down to the poor part of town
and into Le Coq's little hut where he drops it in the center of the
floor.

The procession had both begun in the church and led back into
it again, even as the concept of repaying God by penances was not
original to Le Coq; he had been taught it in the church and the
teaching acted like a boomerang in him. He might stray away but,
sooner or later, need would arise and he would call on God and
then have to repay and it was through the church that payment
was made.

But man is weak and vulnerable and he cannot adequately pay.
He thinks he can measure the stone and handle it, but it is a 'stone
that grows' and becomes too much for him. The chief of police got
drunk and couldn't fulfil his duties properly. Le Coq drank too
much and danced too much also and he couldn't fulfil his promise.

The judgment of the absurd society descended upon the former and of his religious friends upon the latter. When the stone fell from Le Coq's head and he fell with it, "those who were leading the way for him and encouraging him rushed back shouting; one of them took hold of the pad of ivy while the others took up the stone in order to load Le Coq with it again." (CT, 1681) How anxious and concerned they are that he should repay; that he was exhausted physically and emotionally meant nothing to them. They seemed quite unconscious that their attitude added enormously to his load, crushing him spiritually too.

D'Arrast had intervened and prevented his countrymen from wreaking vengeance upon the chief of police but with Le Coq he goes further. He picks up the stone and carries it himself thereby fulfilling his promise for him but then, in turning brusquely aside from the direction of the church and carrying the stone to Le Coq's home, he delivers him from the whole system of superstitious fear and repeated experiences of impossible debt which would only have strengthened their grip on the little man had he carried the stone into the church. D'Arrast leads him out of religion and religious institutions and into the home; and here Camus is prophetic of the spiritual movement of our day. Quite recently a prominent theologian stated publicly his conviction that the years immediately ahead are going to see a widespread migration out of the religious institutions back to simple meetings in the home as in the days of the early church, away from formality back to reality.

The group of short stories, in which *The Stone which Grows* is found, is called *The Exile and the Kingdom;* and there is no doubt that Camus is speaking about the Kingdom of men here and not of God. Yet the relationship between Le Coq and D'Arrast is a spiritual one, they are constantly talking together about the verities of man. The significance of what D'Arrast accomplishes for Le Coq is spiritual, profoundly so, also. We thus are faced with the enigma of Camus's kingdom of men being founded upon spiritual principles and the religious institutions of which he writes being hotbeds of superstitious fear and fetishism. It is a fact that occupation with religion does not necessarily imply something spiritual; unhappily it usually implies the contrary. The adjective 'religious' appears once in the New Testament; the Greek word from which it is translated also means superstitious, as if the two meanings were related

— and indeed they are! "Ye men of Athens" said Paul on Mars Hill "in all things I perceive that you are somewhat religious." (*Acts, 17.22*) The Athenians had erected an altar to 'The Unknown God'; their objective occupation with theories about him is religious and their fear of the unknown about him is superstitious. The Greek noun from which this adjective is derived is never used in the New Testament concerning Christianity which, in its original and real form, is not a religion in that it neither deals with theories of God nor inculcates fear. It is used, however, of Judaism; Paul speaks of his "manner of life in times past in the Jews' religion." (*Galatians, 1.13*)

It is religion that Meursault encounters in the prison chaplain and it is this that evokes a violent reaction in him. The chaplain's strategy is to seek to bring Meursault under condemnation, to get him to break, to weep, to repent; he imputes guilt and judgment and Meursault has to fight him off. But, before we launch into a study of this, there is, I believe, a false impression which may have been given to those who have read only the English translation of *The Stranger* and which should be rectified. The point at which Meursault can take it no longer and explodes is when the chaplain says to him: "I shall pray for you." To which he replies, and here I quote the English translation of Mr. Stuart Gilbert, "...I told him not to waste his rotten prayers on me. It was better to burn than to disappear." (CS, 151) This phrase "...it was better to burn than to disappear," evidently featured in the first edition, was subsequently eliminated; the phrase immediately preceding it needs clarification. The original French reads quite simply "I told him not to pray for me." (Je lui ai dit de ne pas prier). (CT, 1208) If this one correction is made, Meursault's entire outburst will be found to concern a repulsion of the chaplain and the religious system he represented; there are no bitter or resentful jabs against God, prayer, or spiritual verities. He is simply comparing the things he knew, the facts of the life he had lived, with the theories of this religious practitioner. Admittedly he speaks with fervor, but, under the circumstances, that is not hard to understand. On two occasions only does he mention God — the first time there seems to be a trace of sarcasm: "He (the chaplain) wanted to speak further to me about God but I went up close to him and made a final effort to explain to him that I didn't have much time left and I didn't want

to waste it on God." (CT, 1208) The second instance probably goes far in explaining what he meant by 'God' in the first: "of what consequence was *his* God to me?" (CT, 1208)

The outburst was provoked by the chaplain asking Meursault why he called him 'monsieur' instead of 'father'. "That irritated me still more," said Meursault," and I told him he wasn't my father; quite the contrary, he was in with the others — on their side. 'No, my son', he said, putting his hand on my shoulder, 'I'm on your side though you don't realise it because your heart is hardened. But I shall pray for you." The lawyers, judges, the examining magistrate, the director of the old people's home, and others had combined against him to judge him. They were together in an absurd group from which he was excluded and ostracized by judgment. Meursault simply tries to explain that the chaplain is with the judges and the others, that he comes to Meursault requiring him to repent — thus has assumed his guilt and has already judged him. Meursault realised that if he would just bow down, break and confess, then he would be accepted by the absurd, included; in a subservient role, of course! To Yanek of *The Just Assassins* the Grand Duchess also seemed to be 'of the others, in with them,' and not really with him. (CT, 374)

Now the interesting thing concerning all this is that the only occasions recorded in the New Testament on which the wrath of Jesus Christ was aroused were when He came face to face with religionists and their legality and lust for judgment. "He spoke softly to the adulteress" says Clamence in *The Fall,* speaking of the occasion when the woman taken in adultery was brought into the presence of Jesus Christ early in the morning in the Temple. (CF, 115) He did not even speak harshly to Judas Iscariot but sought to help him right up to the very last moment. But He certainly did not speak softly to the Scribes and Pharisees: "Woe unto you, Scribes and Pharisees... ye blind guides... ye fools and blind... hypocrites." He does not mince words with them! On another occasion He went into the Temple and made a scourge of cords and "cast out of the Temple, both the sheep and the oxen: and he poured out the changers' money and overthrew their tables." (*John*, 2.15) It seems that the two most despicable things to Him, which He would not tolerate, were religion masquerading and seeking to gain power over men, and religion being used by those with an eye for business

who turned it to personal profit. It was against these two alone that He exhibited violence, denouncing them in strong, unequivocal terms.

Both of these two aspects are visible in this chaplain: he is a protagonist of an absurd religious system and earns his living by performing those functions. It is most significant to observe that this is the sole occasion in all the works of Camus where one of his principal characters withstands another person and forcefully speaks out against what he represents. At least in this Meursault can be called a Christ figure. The reader may feel that I have been harsh in my treatment of this unfortunate chaplain; much more will be said concerning him in a later chapter where a redeeming feature or two about him will be noted.

Thus the revolt of Meursault is against the absurd in religion. He can do nothing about the absurd in society and its judgment of him, but he can and does resist it violently when it comes to him clad in religious garb and seeking to smother him or "dupe him with its opium," as Karl Marx would say.

8

Absurd Religion

Quite frequently in literature a simpleton, an eccentric or naïve person, or a drunk is used by an author to speak blatantly about some controversial subject in a manner which would not have been fitting for the other more 'normal' characters. The device enables the author to remain hidden, in a measure, whilst freeing him to say exactly what he wants without reservation.

Clamence of *The Fall* certainly falls into the category of eccentric: he looks like a rugby player and yet has his nails manicured; he is also very fond of gin and doubtless spends much of his time under its influence. There is something unsavory about him; towards the end of the book he develops a fever and there is the sense that his sickness extends beyond the physical; nevertheless one can perceive from his words that he has a deep insight into the nature of man and life in general. His speech is not straightforward: "It's very hard to disentangle the true from the false in what I am saying — I admit you are right," he says, and adds "don't lies eventually lead to the truth? And don't all my stories, true or false, tend toward the same conclusion?" (CF, 119)

The Fall is permeated with the foggy atmosphere of Amsterdam. It is also a book of mirrors and, for the most part, one cannot be sure whether it is the voice of Camus that is being heard directly or if the subject is being presented obliquely, reflected through the fictional personality of Clamence. But, when the subject of Jesus

Christ comes up, it seems that the fog lifts, the clouds roll away, the mirror vanishes, and it could only be Camus himself that we hear.

When Clamence broaches the subject of Christianity, he goes at once to the root of the matter and demonstrates the difference between what there was on the earth for three years when the founder walked here and what has subsequently come into being — something spiritual and real on the one hand and religion on the other. "God's sole usefulness would be to guarantee innocence," he says with characteristic sweeping generalisation, "and I am inclined to see religion as a huge laundering venture—as it was once briefly, for exactly three years, and it wasn't called religion. Since then, soap has been lacking, our faces are dirty, and we wipe one another's noses. All dunces, all punished, let's all spit on one another and — hurry! ... Each tries to spit first, that's all. I'll tell you a big secret, my dear fellow. Don't wait for the last judgment. It takes place every day." (CF, 111) For three years there was soap and those who lived in that day experienced being washed but, since then, the soap has been lacking; there has been a performance but it has not produced a salutary effect — the performance is religion.

The big distinction between those three years and what has followed is that "He, my friend ... simply wanted to be loved, nothing more"; whereas they who followed "have hoisted Him onto a judge's bench, in the secret of their hearts, and they smite, they judge above all, they judge in His name." (CF, 115) The contrast between these two diametrically different forces is seen so clearly when they encounter one another in the incident of the woman taken in adultery: "He spoke softly to the adultress — 'Neither do I condemn thee!'—but that doesn't matter; they condemn without absolving anyone. In the Name of the Lord, here is what you deserve." (CF, 115)

It was early in the morning and Jesus had gone into the Temple; a great crowd had gathered and He was teaching them. There was a commotion at the door — some Scribes and Pharisees enter dragging a woman and, making a way for themselves through the assembled gathering, they "set her in the midst." (*John*, 8.3) Their words betray their motives and the lengths to which they are prepared to go in order to reach their objective: "this woman hath been taken in adultery, in the very act." He had been walking amongst them for perhaps two years at this time, not judging but healing;

and His life and reality had made their religious system look obsolete and dead. They had tried to find some point on which they could judge Him and thereby gain the upper hand but, at every encounter, they had found themselves up against an authority in Him which, though inexplicable, was irresistible. They determined to catch Him and devised what must have seemed to be a foolproof scheme. They would send out accomplices to sound out the gossip of the neighborhood to ascertain where they could find a woman actually committing adultery. They would lie in wait and then, picking their time, pounce in and catch her "in the very act." Others of their cohorts would keep track of the whereabouts of Jesus so that, immediately, they could drag her into His presence; then they would present Him with their question: Should they stone her as they were commanded in the Law of Moses? Well did they know that Roman Law forbade stoning for any cause; thus they would have Him cornered and, whichever way He answered, would be able to judge Him by one law or the other. Little did they anticipate the higher wisdom they were to encounter: "He that is without sin among you, let him cast the first stone at her." According to the record, when they heard this they went out one by one, beginning from the eldest, even unto the last! Being left alone with the woman, Jesus said to her: "Woman, where are they? Did no man condemn thee?" and she replied "No man, Lord." Jesus said to her: Neither do I condemn thee; go thy way; from henceforth sin no more."

There was certainly soap on that day as that woman would doubtless have affirmed, going from His presence morally and spiritually washed clean. Then what went wrong subsequently that the soap ran out? "They have hoisted Him onto a judge's bench, in the secret of their hearts, and they smite, they judge above all, they judge in His Name." How short a time it was after those three years were over that man largely forgot their meaning. The words which, when first uttered, had meant life and illumination to those who heard, were formed into yet another system which could be applied as a standard of morality and thus a basis for judgment; and the cross, which had been the ultimate in humiliation for Him, became a ladder upon which "too many people now climb merely to be seen from a greater distance even if they have to trample somewhat on the one who has been there so long." (CF, 114) Thus the reli-

gion that Christianity developed into satisfied the pride of man in two ways. It provided him with a ladder to success, a means by which he could 'get ahead' if he wished to take it up as a career or, if he preferred just to have its security without carrying any of the responsibility for it as a movement, it provided a system of morality which would give him a feeling of well-being and belonging as he subscribed to it and a sense of being above as he used it as a basis upon which to judge others.

But what is even more absurd is that Christianity has divided up into multiple denominations, each with its own system of teachings which provides for its adherents both the security of a fold and some kind of basis upon which they can claim superiority over the others. Very often the absurdity of a particular denomination has close ties with the absurd social realm of the most part of its members. It is no accident that in England, for instance, the middle and upper classes vote conservative and belong to the Church of England whereas the lower classes vote 'labor' and belong to some non-conformist denomination.

In the West we have lived with this doubly absurd situation of multiple denominations for so long that our consciences have become dulled to its absurdity. We have even learnt how to make excuses for it; we say it represents variety and that all tastes are catered for and we exhort people to "attend the church of their choice." Little do we know how clearly others see through us. I want to recount, as an illustration of this, what some Chinese friends of mine told me of the early days of Communist occupation of their land and how the Communists dealt with the 'religious problem.'

When they first took over China, shortly after World War II, the Communists evidently assured all the denominations that they wanted everyone to be perfectly free to continue to worship how and where he wished and that they had no intention of tampering with people's beliefs. This news was received of course with delight by believers of all faiths; and those who, when the Communists first arrived, had been fearful and had withdrawn from church services, became more courageous and went back again. But after two years there came a change of policy; the Communists announced that they were shocked by the different brands of Christianity — how could there be divergent teachings and practices, they

asked? They insisted that in the utopia they were building there was no place for religious schisms which were a contradiction. If the different Christian denominations wished to continue, they said, they must join together and cooperate and form one religion! A bitter pill to swallow to be told by the Communists, of all people, that your denominational differences are a contradiction! As the denominations seemed incapable of effecting this unity, the communists informed them that they would assist in the matter. They established what they called a central committee at the head of which they placed a liberal-minded minister who was also a Communist sympathiser, and they announced that any group which wished to continue in existence should send a representative to this committee. It was then a simple matter for the Communists to dictate what could be preached in churches and what could not. For instance, they forbade all preaching about 'this present evil world' for, said they, we are not going to have an evil world when we have finished with it but an Utopia. The total depravity of man was something else which could not be mentioned for Mao was not depraved. The divinity of Jesus Christ was absolutely forbidden: if He ever existed He was just a man, according to them.

By this master move, the Communists managed to take the very heart and Gospel out of the churches. To accomplish this they had used the contradiction of the plurality of denominations to take the moral ground from under the feet of the Christians who, in their divided state, found themselves defenseless. This was not all; their subtlety went even deeper. During those first years, when they said that they wanted everyone to continue in perfect freedom of worship, the fearful weak believers, who had withdrawn from the churches on the arrival of the Communists, became a little bolder, returned to the services, and their names were recorded on the rolls. But, when the central committee was formed, these ones began to slip away again, hoping to remain uninvolved. The communists knew this would happen, waited for it and then made an announcement that it was not right for people to slip away like that; all whose names were on the rolls should continue to attend. So the fearful were forced back to the services, more fearful than ever! It can be imagined that whatever influence they exerted, once they were back in the fold, was towards cooperation at any cost with the dictates of the government.

There was another incident, a few years after what has been recorded above, which demonstrates even more deeply the profound spiritual or moral understanding of the communists. There was a movement which, on account of its independent status and free loose affiliation, being somewhat more of a flock than a fold, survived the measures described above for the elimination of true Christianity. The Communists observed this and plotted its downfall. On a certain Sunday they took into custody the principal workers, hundreds of them, all over China. Those who were at the heart of the work, about eight persons, were taken to a special prison in Shanghai where they were interrogated individually. The surprising thing to them was that the interrogation took the same form for each one of them. They were each asked to criticize or judge just one of their fellow workers. It wasn't necessary to find some serious fault, a little thing would do just so long as they would judge another—if they would do this, they would be set free! It should be recorded that none of these workers would do this; each independently said that he could not possibly criticize his brother who had been taken in hand by God to be conformed to the image of Christ. Why did the Communists make this offer? The answer is that they have a deep understanding of the operation of the principle of judgment and the absurd. They know that if A can persuade B to judge C, then two things are accomplished—the relationship between B and C is marred if not broken and B finds himself with a kind of moral obligation to A, he has come under his authority.

This was the nature of the struggle of the Janitor of the Old People's home during the court case. The assembled absurd was calling upon him to judge the defendant and fear drove him to comply until, struck by the kindness and selflessness of Meursault, he pulled himself together, took the bull by the horns and threw off this ogre of sinister authority which was oppressing him. The communists could and would, of course, have used anything any of the workers might have said against another as evidence against that person, but this was quite secondary. They knew that a kind of moral dependence was created between a system and any person whom that system could persuade to judge another on its behalf. The person who is judged is not affected morally in himself although he may be punished—his integrity is not touched. But the person who is tricked into doing the judging loses his moral ground,

although quite unwittingly perhaps. How alarming it is to hear that in the United States the same kind of mechanism is being employed under the name of 'Sensitivity Training'. Just the other day an incident was recounted to the author in which the faculty of a public school were instructed to sit in a circle, join hands, and criticize the principal, who was seated in the center of the circle. He was evidently broken by the experience and is out of teaching this academic year; but what happened to those who collaborated in the judging? They have, unknowingly I hope, given their allegiance to a system, in a measure sold themselves morally to those who asked them to participate in the affair. The principal may be broken but, in a sense, theirs is a worse plight; they have forfeited their independent moral manhood. The Janitor in the court scene of *The Stranger* was not in too deep and thus was able to extricate himself; had he been in a little deeper it might have been well nigh impossible for him to get out and remain free.

It must be around twenty-five years now since all this took place in China. Happily there is another side to the story; there have been all along and still are groups which meet in secret where true believers have the comfort of being for brief moments with others of like faith. What a lot has happened in twenty-five years, however! Talk of denominational differences seems almost out of date today! Most groups are scurrying to get together as quickly as possible. It was even suggested the other day at a conference on the Eastern Seaboard that a group of denominations, currently talking of unity, take the plunge and unite right away and leave the theologians to sort out the doctrinal niceties later on! Such an attitude proves that the principles for which these groups once stood are no longer of real consequence. They all share in one common principle—morality. "Take our moral philosophers, for instance," says Clamence, "so serious, loving their neighbor and all the rest—nothing distinguishes them from Christians except that they don't preach in churches." (CF, 133) Earlier in the book he says, "Believe me, religions are on the wrong track the moment they moralize and fulminate commandments." (CF, 110) And yet, for the most part, what else does the Church in the West have left in these days? In his book *Protestant - Catholic - Jew* Will Herberg says: "It is only too evident that the religiousness characteristic of America to-day is very often a religiousness without religion, a

religiousness with almost any kind of content or none, a way of sociability or 'belonging' rather than a way of reorienting life to God. It is thus frequently a religiousness without serious commitment, without real inner conviction . . . the Unknown God of Americans is faith itself. What Americans believe in when they are religious is religion itself. Of course Americans speak of God and Christ but what they seem to regard as really redemptive is primarily religion, the 'positive' attitude of believing. It is this faith in faith, this religion which makes religion its own object, that is the outstanding characteristic of contemporary American religiosity. Daniel Poling's formula: 'I began saying in the morning two words —I believe—those two words with nothing added' may be taken as the classic expression of this aspect of American faith." (HP, 260, 265)

Perhaps it is the hollowness, unreality, and superficiality of such a state which causes Camus to assume a bitter, almost cynical tone when he speaks of the two great doctrines concerning the Christian's salvation, namely redemption and santification. Speaking of Jesus Christ, Clamence says: "People naturally tried to get some help from His death. After all, it was a stroke of genius to tell us: 'You are not a very pretty sight, that's certain! Well we won't go into the details! We'll just liquidate it all at once, on the cross!' " (CF, 114) This is the doctrine of redemption from the guilt of sins. The doctrine of Sanctification is touched upon by the young missionary in *The Renegade*, of all people, before going out to his station: "Finally I too wanted to be an example," he says, "So that others might look upon me and, in seeing me, give glory to the One who had changed me for the better; so that through me others might see and recognize my Lord." (CT, 1578) Far from accomplishing this, he is converted by the evil vicious tribe to whom he went and ends up fearing their fetish and worshipping hate. He murders the old missionary who is sent out to replace him and finally experiences remorse as he sees grace in the face of the old man dying. Why should Camus have put these two gems of the Christian faith into the mouths of his two characters who were respectively the most dissolute—Clamence, and the most confused —the young missionary in *The Renegade*? Is it not most probably because feeling, as we know he did, that Christians do little or nothing to seek to deal with the root of the malady, pride, he

thought that they used these teachings as an excuse or an escape from reality to quieten their consciences, only too willing to look no further into the matter—"Well, we won't go into the details!"

Clamence, on the other hand, has a fascination for the subject and recounts an experience which befell him in North Africa to illustrate the strength of pride as the cohesive force of absurd institutions. He found himself "interned near Tripoli in a camp where we suffered from thirst and destitution more than from brutality." (CF, 123) Amongst their number was a young Frenchman, ardent of faith, who "declared to us the need for a new pope who should live among the wretched instead of praying on a throne, and the sooner the better. . . . He said that we must choose him among us, pick a complete man with his vices and virtues and swear allegiance to him, on the sole condition that he should keep alive, in himself and in others, the community of our sufferings. 'Who among us,' he asked, 'has the most failings?' As a joke I raised my hand and was the only one to do so. . . . He declared that nominating oneself as I had done presupposed also the greatest virtue and proposed electing me. The others agreed, in fun, but with a trace of seriousness all the same." (CF, 125)

The main problem in the camp was the allocation of the drinking water and this task fell to Clamence as pope. His great difficulty was to remain impartial and he found it well nigh impossible not to favor his personal friends. "Among us, according to my comrades' condition, or the work they had to do, I gave an advantage to this one or that one. Such distinctions are far-reaching. . . . I closed the circle (tied the whole thing up) the day I drank the water of a dying comrade. . . . I drank the water . . . convincing myself that the others needed me more than this fellow who was going to die anyway and that I had a duty to keep myself alive for them. Thus empires and churches are born under the sun of death." (CF, 126-27)

In a few simple phrases, here, Clamence has set forth a process which, once set in motion, develops irrevocably along definite lines to produce a certain end. There is a group of men who are locked in together in such circumstances that the sun, whose warmth normally produces growth, is oppressive to them, causing suffering and need. In this predicament, seeking some way to ease their trials, the men appoint a leader, half-jokingly at first, but soon discover that

their act has far more significance than they could possibly have imagined. The leader is forced to use his own judgment which he discovers is not impartial; and his decisions create alliances and distinctions which are far-reaching. He grows progressively in a sense of his own importance to the group to such an extent that, one day, rather than giving the usual water ration to a man who was about to die anyway, he drinks it himself out of a sense of duty to keep himself alive for the others. The circle is closed, the whole thing tied up—the group has become a body of which the leader is the head. This is the progression, he says, by which empires and churches are founded. It is obviously true of dictatorships and empires, but is it true of churches?

A careful examination of the Acts of the Apostles and the letters of the apostle Paul reveals that there were very definite principles which governed the Church at the outset. The Church at Antioch came into being as the result of certain believers travelling and locating there; it is never mentioned that this or that person was the guiding influence in its founding. It was to Antioch that Paul came and thence that he went out on his missionary journeys and, without doubt, the spiritual order or way of doing things at Antioch greatly influenced his thinking. It can be seen that never, on a point of principle, was one man left in charge of a group of believers in a locality; it was always plural—the elders. Nor is there ever any mention of there being a group of elders among whom one was recognised as the senior. They are always regarded as being on an equal footing. The believers at Corinth allowed themselves to be drawn away from this position by their preferences and some said "I am of Paul" and others "I am of Peter" etc. But Peter and Paul would have no part in such a thing and refused to visit them until they had relinquished all personal preferences and come back again onto the right ground of all being no more and no less than 'brothers in Christ'.

There is no place on earth more devastating to human pride than the ground, described above, as practiced in the early church. And that is precisely what it was supposed to be; here is the place where the root of the malady can be dealt with. If a group of individuals gather on this ground, committing themselves to meet and continue together in the belief that God will show his authority amongst them through one and another as He wills, then all human pride

will be undone sooner or later. It must have been very hard for
Peter, who was so greatly respected by all, when he slipped into
a practice which was inconsistent with the message he preached and
was "withstood to the face" by Paul; and what is more, for it to
be done "in the presence of them all." (*Galatians*, 2.11) There was
no official authority in those days, it was either there in spiritual
reality or not at all. Yet Peter can write later in one of his epistles:
"And account that the longsuffering of Our Lord is salvation; even
as our beloved brother Paul also, according to the wisdom given
unto him, wrote unto you." (*2 Peter*, 3.15) How fine is the inclu-
sion of 'beloved' there, he could easily have omitted that! It proves
that there were no residual hard feelings on his side.

Very early in the Church's history, sadly enough, there arose
spiritual circumstances, corresponding to Clamence's physical ones
in the group at Tripoli, in which there was heat and its resultant
problems. Whenever men are confined together, if pride has not
been dealt with, there will be friction and consequently heat! It
was felt that it would be easier and more practical to have a
presiding overseer; decisions would be made more quickly and
simply and 'personality conflicts' would be avoided. Of course! But
the whole purpose of the ground which was to root out the very
essence of the malady of man, pride, was thus lost. It is a great
deal easier to appoint a person in responsibility and then do what
he says, for, after all, you really have the upper hand anyway
because you appointed him, than it is to gather in humility on equal
ground and, with an open heart, seek to come together to what "the
mind of the Lord is."

The elevation of men to offices in churches can only gratify
their pride whilst safeguarding intact the pride of those who elect
them; and one of the fundamental purposes of the Church is
thwarted, namely that "the time is come for judgment (or the
sorting out of things) to begin at the House of God." (*1 Peter*,
4.17) How profound is the discernment of Camus as, through the
medium of Clamence, he says: "I drank the water, convincing
myself that the others needed me more than this fellow who was
going to die anyway and that I had a duty to keep myself alive for
them. Thus empires and churches are born under the sun of death."
No wonder, having seen all this, Clamence concludes. "My great
idea is that we must forgive the pope. To begin with, he needs it

more than anyone else." He adds a parting thrust with a characteristic humor and an eye which is ever on the alert to the outlet for
personal pride: "Secondly, that's the only way to set oneself above
him!" (CF, 127)

9

The Malady in Service

Before launching into a detailed study of the three principal characters in the works of Camus who engage in the propagation of Christianity, it is necessary first, for a few moments, to return to the subject of the first chapter and refresh our minds as to the distinction between what is spiritual and what is not.

"The spirit does not occupy itself with things," said Saint-Exupéry, "but rather with the sense or meaning which ties them together—it is another face which lies back of them. The spirit passes from full and open vision to absolute blindness." (SO, 275) A distinction between the soul and the spirit, as those terms are used in this study, is that the various aspects of the soul life in the man are always accessible to him and could exercise themselves at any moment if let loose by him, whereas the spirit is a consciousness over which he has less control, it seems to come more from outside the man when the turbulence of his soul is sufficiently calmed to receive it: he cannot get it but he can seek to quieten his soul so that it may come. Towards the end of *The Fall*, Clamence sees snowflakes or doves descending upon Amsterdam; in the Scriptures the Spirit descended like a dove also—something from outside the man which conveys to him a higher, broader understanding and consciousness than is possible to his confined and limited soul.

If the spirit is that deeper understanding which comes to man when his soul is stilled, that other face which lies back of things

83

which can so quickly be frightened away should the soul catch fire on any issue, then how can the soul be defined? It is the sum of those capacities in man which are at his disposal and which he may use to attain his goals. We call it immaturity when they control him and maturity when he controls them. These capacities can be divided up into three main categories; first: volition, which may exercise itself as will power, determination, or ambition; second: the whole realm of the emotions, anger, fear, love, hate; and third: reason. These may operate independently or together. The successful politician, for example, will have to know how to mingle the emotional appeal with the logical demonstration of his case and, back of his presentation, there must be strength of will and self-confidence to convey conviction. It seems that Camus knew all of this and deliberately chose to portray one of these aspects of the soul life in each of the three principal Christian protagonists he created.

The Examining Magistrate of *The Stranger* is overbearing and domineering. Meursault, to him, is just a candidate for conversion and he meets him head-on objectively; he uses will and the force of personality. The Prison Chaplain of *The Stranger* is much more subtle; he uses the emotional approach, which one feels is downright dishonest as it is controlled by a sort of psychoanalytic dexterity, cat and mouse style, behind the scenes. In Paneloux, the Jesuit priest of *The Plague,* we see reason. Now to examine each one separately.

After accidentally killing a man, Meursault is imprisoned and spends some months being questioned whilst his case is prepared for trial. A conversation that he had with his lawyer at this period has been recounted earlier in the chapter on *The Absurdity of Life.* The interrogation and preparation of the case is in the hands of the Examining Magistrate who, Meursault notices on their first meeting, "eyed me with distinct curiosity." He describes him as "a tall man with clean-cut features, deep-set blue eyes, a big gray moustache and abundant, almost snow-white hair, and he gave me the impression of being highly intelligent and, on the whole, likeable enough. There was only one thing that put me off; his mouth had now and then a rather ugly twist; but it seemed to be only a sort of nervous tic." (CS, 77)

During their second interview Meursault began to notice that this

man was different from the lawyer, who was only interested in the case for what he could get from it. The Examining Magistrate spoke directly: " ' What really interests me is you!' he said, leaning suddenly forward, looking me in the eyes and raising his voice a little." Then, after a few more enquiries "he stood up and said he'd like to help me; I interested him, and, with God's help, he would do something for me in my trouble." (CS, 83) But first he had some more enquiries to make, the main one being as to why Meursault had continued to fire on the prostrate Arab who had been killed by the first bullet; but this was just what he could not answer as he, himself, did not know why he did it; hence he said nothing. "During the silence that followed, the Magistrate kept fidgeting, running his fingers through his hair, half rising, then sitting down again. . . . Suddenly he rose, walked to a file cabinet standing against the opposite wall, pulling a drawer open, and took from it a silver crucifix, which he was waving as he came back to the desk. "Do you know who this is?" His voice had changed completely; it was vibrant with emotion. "Of course I do," I answered. That seemed to start him off; he began speaking at a great pace. He told me that he believed in God, and that even the worst of sinners could obtain forgiveness from Him. But he must first repent, and become like a little child, with a simple trustful heart, open to conviction. He was leaning right across the table, brandishing his crucifix before my eyes. . . . He drew himself up to his full height and was asking me if I believed in God. When I said 'No', he plumped down in his chair indignantly."

"That was unthinkable, he said; all men believe in God, even those who reject Him. Of this he was absolutely sure; if he ever came to doubt it, his life would lose all meaning. 'Do you wish,' he asked indignantly, 'my life to have no meaning?' Really I couldn't see how my wishes came into it, and I told him as much. While I was talking, he thrust a crucifix under my nose and shouted 'I, anyhow, am a Christian. And I pray Him to forgive you for your sins. My poor young man, how can you not believe that He suffered for your sake?' I noticed that his manner seemed genuinely solicitous when he said 'my poor young man'—but I was beginning to have enough of it. The room was growing steadily hotter. As I usually do when I want to get rid of someone whose conversation bores me, I pretended to agree. At which, rather to my surprise,

his face lit up. 'You see! You see! Now won't you own that you believe and put your trust in Him?' I must have shaken my head again, for he sank back in his chair, looking limp and dejected. . . . He looked at me intently and rather sadly. 'Never in all my experience have I known a soul so case-hardened as yours,' he said in a low tone. 'All the criminals who have come before me until now wept when they saw this symbol of Our Lord's sufferings.' " (CS, 84-7)

Meursault recounts how, from this time, the sessions with his lawyer and Examining Magistrate seemed to change tone. They confined themselves to asking him to amplify his previous statements. "The Magistrate seemed to have lost interest in me," he says, "and to have come to some sort of decision about my case. He never mentioned God again or displayed any of the religious fervor I had found so embarrassing at our first interview. The result was that our relations became more cordial. . . . I can honestly say that, during the last eleven months these examinations lasted, I got so used to them that I was almost surprised at having ever enjoyed anything better than those rare moments when the magistrate, after escorting me to the door of his office, would pat me on the shoulder and say in a friendly tone: 'Well! Mr. Antichrist, that's all for the present!' After which I was made over to my jailers." (CS, 88)

Here is a man of the intense type who, once he has been convinced of the truth of a thing, cannot understand why others do not immediately see as he. He is unable to listen sympathetically. He asks questions so that he may be able to categorize his respondent by his replies, or to lead him on to a conclusion he has foreseen. He says: "What really interests me is you!" But in reality that is not the case. Meursault is only of interest to him so long as there seems to be a chance of his being won over and, when that has gone, "the magistrate seemed to have lost interest in me."

This is the sort of man who, if he got involved in politics, would be extreme one way or the other. If he held a position as a salesman, he would intimidate his buyers into purchasing. If he taught school, there would not be many questions asked in his classes! Even as the lawyer needed cases to provide him the means for 'getting ahead', so this magistrate thrived on thrusting upon others, through the force of his personality and will power, his convictions on

spiritual truths. But were those others really convinced? "All the criminals who have come before me until now wept when they saw this symbol of Our Lord's sufferings." There is not necessarily a connection between tears and spiritual conviction! Man weeps quite easily when stirred emotionally, and he can be stirred in so many ways; a play, a piece of music, a sad story, self-pity. All who came before this magistrate were doubtless not far from tears anyway. He had them at a disadvantage; they were cornered. There were certainly some who thought that a good display of emotion might weigh in their favor when the case came before the court. These criminals were a captive audience—sitting ducks! Fundamentally this magistrate thrusts himself upon them thus, not because he is really concerned for their souls' destiny but because every time he manages to produce the effect he is looking for in one of them, this gratifies him. Indeed, he positively "needs" to succeed or his faith would be weakened. "Do you wish my life to have no meaning?" he asks Meursault (CS, 86), as if the latter's decision in this matter of believing would vitally affect his own faith. If he could have persuaded Meursault, this would have given him a sense of having accomplished his duty, of being justified. The whole affair put an intolerable strain on Meursault: "The room was growing steadily hotter." (CS, 86)

Those whose driving force in spiritual service is will power have the ability to recover quickly from a setback; they are more superficial than the other two mentioned in this chapter, and more innocuous, certainly, than the emotional type.

If all this seems too harsh and unfair towards this unfortunate Examining Magistrate, two quotes from La Rochefoucauld restore the balance. "We would often be ashamed of our most beautiful actions if everyone was to see the motives which produced them"; and, on the other side of the coin, "Self-interest, which one accuses of all crimes, often merits to be praised for our good actions." (RO, 305, 290)

The prison chaplain of *The Stranger* is altogether different. His objective is the same as that of the Examining Magistrate but his way of going about it is quite other. The Magistrate was brute force and met his prey head-on; the chaplain is much more subtle, he plucks at the heartstrings behind Meursault's back. The Magistrate just wants to extricate a verbal confession of belief from his victim

by the quickest and shortest route possible; this chaplain wants to do the same thing but he is more sensitive, he works by suggestion, inference, and an appeal to the imagination. In short, his approach is psychological.

Meursault had been condemned to death by the court and he is waiting in his cell from day to day either for news of a retrial or reprieve, or for the footstep of the executioner to come to his door one day at dawn. He is meditating as to the possibility of an escape when, all of a sudden, "the chaplain walked in unannounced. I couldn't help giving a start on seeing him. He noticed this evidently, as he promptly told me not to be alarmed. I reminded him that usually his visits were at another time, and for a pretty grim occasion. This, he replied, was just a friendly visit; it had no concern with my appeal, about which he knew nothing. Then he sat on my bed, asking me to sit beside him. I refused—not because I had anything against him; he seemed a mild, amiable man."

"He remained quite still at first, his arms resting on his knees, his eyes fixed on his hands. They were slender but sinewy hands, which made me think of two nimble animals. Then he gently rubbed them together. He stayed so long in the same position that for a while I almost forgot he was there.

"All of a sudden he jerked his head up and looked me in the eyes. 'Why,' he asked, 'Don't you let me come to see you?' I explained that I didn't believe in God. 'Are you really so sure of that?' I said I saw no point in troubling my head about the matter; whether I believed or didn't was, to my mind, a question of so little importance. He leaned back against the wall, laying his hands flat on his thighs. Almost without seeming to address me, he remarked that he'd often noticed one fancies that one is quite sure about something when, in point of fact, one isn't. When I said nothing, he looked at me again, and asked 'Don't you agree?' " (CS, 144)

This is no frontal assault like that of the magistrate, it is altogether more subtle. It is the attempt to probe the psyche of Meursault to find a weak spot he could play on. When it is apparent that he has made no progress down this line, he shifts tactics. " 'If you don't die soon, you'll die one day. And then the same question will arise. How will you face that terrible final hour?' I replied that I'd face it exactly as I was facing it now. Thereat he stood up,

and looked me straight in the eyes. It was a trick I well knew. I used to amuse myself trying it on Emmanuel and Celeste, and nine times out of ten they'd look away uncomfortably. I could see the chaplain was an old hand at it, as his gaze never faltered. And his voice was quite steady when he said: 'Have you no hope at all? Do you really think that when you die you die outright, and nothing remains?' I said: 'Yes'. He dropped his eyes and sat down again. He was truly sorry for me, he said. It must make life unbearable for a man, to think as I did." (CS, 147) As this tack fails, he tries yet another.

"Slowly the priest gazed around my cell, and I was struck by the sadness of his voice when he replied: 'These stone walls, I know it only too well, are steeped in human suffering. I've never been able to look at them without a shudder. And yet—believe me, I am speaking from the depths of my heart—I know that even the wretchedest among you have sometimes seen, taking form against that grayness, a divine face. It's that face you are asked to see.' This roused me a little. I informed him that I'd been staring at those walls for months; there was nobody, nothing in the world, I knew better than I knew them. . . . I had no luck, I'd never seen anything 'taking form', as he called it, against those walls.

"The chaplain gazed at me with a sort of sadness. I now had my back to the wall and light was flowing over my forehead. He muttered some words I didn't catch; then abruptly asked if he might kiss me. I said 'No'. Then he turned, came to the wall, and slowly drew his hand along it. 'Do you really love these earthly things so much?' he asked in a low voice." (CS, 148)

How difficult it is to cope with a man like this who refuses to be put off! Meursault says "I had my back to the wall"; but still this man goes after him probing from one direction after another. This is much harder to endure than the magistrate who pours it all out in one flood and then, if it doesn't work, gives up. Of course the magistrate is a magistrate and has that type of work to do; this chaplain, on the other hand, these conversations are his work, so it can be understood that he does not give up so easily. His approach wavers between hypnotism—"He looked me straight in the eyes"; mysticism—"These stone walls. . . . I know that even the wretchedest amongst you have sometimes seen, taking form against that grayness, a divine face"; and a nauseating kind of emotionalism

—"He muttered some words I didn't catch; then abruptly asked if he might kiss me." Meursault could tolerate the Magistrate and his direct frontal assault even if "the room was growing steadily hotter"; (CS, 86) but there was something unclean, evil about this chaplain playing on his emotions. No wonder, as he felt "his back to the wall," a revolt was aroused in him and he burst out in a bitter diatribe against this man. For the chaplain, we should not let pass unnoticed that, when he left the cell, there were tears in his eyes; it would be charitable to assume that, at this juncture, he had laid aside the role he had been playing and the tears were genuine.

The priest of *The Plague*, Father Paneloux by name, is different again. It is neither will power and force of personality nor psychology with him. He is governed by reason and, in the delivery of his sermons, he is an orator.

"The first month of the plague ended gloomily, with a violent recrudescence of the epidemic and a dramatic sermon preached by Father Paneloux, the Jesuit priest," recounts the narrator. "Father Paneloux had already made his mark with frequent contributions to the Oran Geographical society; these dealt chiefly with ancient inscriptions, on which he was an authority. But he also reached a wider, non-specialist public with a series of lectures on present-day individualism. In these he had shown himself a stalwart champion of Christian Doctrine at its most precise and purest, equally remote from modern laxity and the obscurantism of the past. On these occasions he had not shrunk from trouncing his hearers with some vigorous home-truths. Hence his celebrity." (CP, 84)

He was a student and a reasoned thinker, being a Jesuit, and quite fearless about speaking out his mind. It fell his lot to deliver the sermon which would conclude a week of prayer on account of the plague. "The air inside the cathedral was heavy with fumes of incense and the smell of wet clothes when Father Paneloux stepped into the pulpit. He was a stockily built man, of medium height. When he leaned on the pulpit, grasping the woodwork with his big hands, all one saw was a black, massive torso and, above it, two rosy cheeks overhung by steel-rimmed spectacles. He had a powerful, rather emotional delivery, which carried to a great distance, and when he launched at the congregation his opening phrase in

clear, emphatic tones—'Calamity has come on you, my brethren, and, my brethren, you deserved it'—there was a flutter that extended to the crowd massed in the rain outside the porch. In strict logic, what came next did not seem to follow from this dramatic opening. Only as the sermon proceeded did it become apparent to the congregation that, by a skilful oratorical device, Father Paneloux had launched at them, like a fisticuff, the gist of his whole discourse." (CP, 86) The essence of his theme is that the plague is a visitation of God upon the inhabitants of Oran because of their sin.

"For a long time God gazed down upon this town with eyes of compassion; but He grew weary of waiting, His eternal hope was too long deferred, and now He has turned His face away from us. And so, God's light withdrawn, we walk in darkness, in the thick darkness of this plague. . . . The just man need have no fear, but the evildoer has good cause to tremble. For the plague is the flail of God and the world is His threshing-floor, and implacably He will thresh out His harvest until the wheat is separated from the chaff. There will be more chaff than wheat, few chosen of the many called." Not very heartening news for the inhabitants of a city whose gates are shut and who are closeted with the plague until it has run its course through their midst!

Paneloux goes on to explain. "You fondly imagined it was enough to visit God on Sundays, and thus you could make free of your weekdays. You believed some brief formalities, some bending of the knees, would recompense Him well enough for your criminal indifference. But God is not mocked. These brief encounters could not sate the fierce hunger of His love. He wished to see you longer and more often; that is his manner of loving and, indeed, it is the only manner of loving. And this is why, wearied of waiting for you to come to Him, He loosed on you this visitation." (CP, 89) The plague is explained as a manifestation of God's love: A somewhat insistent form of it! The effect of all of this was naturally to bring the hearers under condemnation. Did he offer any practical counsel?

"Many of you are wondering, I know, what I am leading up to. I wish to lead you to the truth and teach you to rejoice—in spite of all I have been telling you. This same pestilence which is slaying you works for your good and points your path. . . . The will of God in action unfailingly transforming evil into good. And once again

to-day it is leading us through the dark valley of fears and groans towards the holy silence, the well-spring of life." He adds briefly that "he hoped against hope that, despite the groans of men and women in agony, our fellow-citizens would offer up to heaven that one prayer which is truly Christian, a prayer of love. And God would see to the rest." (CP, 91)

The narrator, Dr. Rieux, recounts that "to some the sermon simply brought home the fact that they had been sentenced, for an unknown crime, to an indeterminate period of punishment." (CP, 92) The hearers were numbed and awed by Paneloux's presentation and were left high and dry by his having nothing practical to offer other than that they pray "the Christian prayer of love," whatever that was! Apart from this one mention of 'Christian Love' there is nothing in the sermon particularly Christian; it could equally well have been preached by anyone of any religion who believed in a God who visited His creatures in judgment because of their unrighteousness. At best it could be called Old Testament, the reasoned application of a law of inexorable justice. Dr. Rieux seems to be on a much more wholesome track when he comments to Tarrou on this sermon: "I've seen too much of hospitals to relish any idea of collective punishment. But, as you know, Christians sometimes say that sort of thing without really thinking it." (CP, 115) It is later in this conversation that the Doctor, who affirms that he does not believe in God, adds: "Mightn't it be better for God if we don't believe in Him and if we struggle with all our might against death, without raising our eyes toward heaven where he sits in silence?" (CP, 117)

So Rieux, Tarrou, and others work together with all their might to save all the lives they can from the plague. They organize groups of workers who look after hospitals, administer quarantine camps, and such tasks. After a while, when it is obvious that the whole city is beset and that there is no one who is a special case and should be permitted to depart, such a person as Rambert, who had been trying to escape and return to his mistress in France, offers himself for the service. Finally Father Paneloux too comes to throw in his lot and cooperate.

The crisis for them all is when the little son of M. Othon falls sick of the plague. They all—Rieux, Tarrou, Rambert, and Paneloux—gather around his bedside as they have tried the new vaccine

on him and much depends on the outcome. "Paneloux, the first to come, leaned against the wall on the opposite side of the bed to Tarrou. His face was drawn with grief; and the accumulated weariness of many weeks, during which he never spared himself, had deeply seamed his somewhat prominent forehead." (CP, 192) They all stayed by the child's bedside throughout the night, witnessing the agony of suffering that accompanies the last stages of the disease. Dr. Castel is there too; it is he who has prepared the new vaccine. "There wasn't any remission this morning, was there, Rieux?" he asks. Rieux shook his head, adding, however, that the child was putting up more resistance than one would have expected. Paneloux, who was slumped against the wall, said in a low voice: "So if he is to die, he will have suffered longer!" (CP, 194)

The climax approaches, "Paneloux gazed down at the small mouth, fouled by the sores of the plague and pouring out the pitiful death cry which has sounded through all the ages of mankind. He sank on his knees, and all present found it natural to hear him say in a voice hoarse but clearly audible across that nameless, never-ending wail: 'My God, spare this child!' " (CP, 195)

It is quite obvious from his ensuing discussion with the doctor that this experience really shook Paneloux. He clearly felt a profound sympathy with Rieux and the others who were fighting the plague, and took his place right out in the forefront of activity with them where he was the most exposed to the infection. The sight of the sufferings of those who were infected coupled with the deep fraternity of those who together labored against the disease, caused him to think again about his spiritual position. "Though theoretically immunised by periodical immunisations, Paneloux was well aware that, at any moment, death might claim him too, and he had given thought to this. Outwardly he had lost nothing of his serenity. But, from the day on which he saw a child die, something seemed to change in him. And his face bore traces of the rising tension of his thoughts. When one day he told Rieux with a smile that he was working on a short essay entitled 'Is a priest jusitfied in consulting a doctor?' Rieux gathered that something graver lay behind the question than the priest's tone seemed to imply. On the doctor's saying that he would greatly like to have a look at the essay, Paneloux informed him that he would shortly be

preaching at a mass for men, and his sermon would convey some
at least of his considered opinions on the question." (CP, 198) He
invited the Doctor to come and hear him preach.

When Rieux arrived at the church it was to notice that it was
nothing like so full as on the previous occasion. As Paneloux opened
his discourse, the doctor observed that "he spoke in a gentler, more
thoughtful tone than on the previous occasion, and several times
stumbled over his words. A yet more noteworthy change was that
instead of addressing his audience 'you,' he now said 'we'." (CP, 200)

The essence of this sermon is that there are times in the
Christian's life when there arise things he cannot understand, things
which seem to be the very opposite from what a God of love would
permit. What was one to do in these circumstances? "My brothers,
a time of testing has come for all of us. We must believe everything
or deny everything. And who among you, I ask, would dare deny
everything? . . . True, the agony of a child was humiliating to the
heart and to the mind. But that was why we had to come to terms
with it. And that, too, was why (and here Paneloux assured those
present that it was not easy to say what he was going to say)
since it was God's will, we, too, should will it. Thus and thus only
the Christian could face the problem squarely and, scorning sub-
terfuge, pierce to the heart of the supreme issue, the essential
choice. And his choice would be to believe everything, so as not to
be forced into denying everything. . . No, there was no middle
course. We must accept the dilemma and choose either to hate God
or to love Him. And who would dare to choose to hate Him?"

Coming to the conclusion of his sermon, Paneloux summed up:
"My brothers, the love of God is a hard love. It demands total self-
surrender, disdain of our human personality. And yet it alone can
reconcile for suffering and the deaths of children, it alone can justify
them, since we cannot understand them and we can only make
God's will ours. That is the hard lesson I would share with you
to-day. That is the faith, cruel in men's eyes, and crucial in God's,
which we must ever strive to compass. We must aspire beyond
ourselves toward that high and fearful vision. And on that lofty
plane all will fall in place, all discords will be resolved, and truth
flash forth from the dark cloud of seeming injustice." (CP, 205)

On leaving the church, Rieux overheard a conversation between
two priests one of whom said he felt the sermon exhibited "more

uneasiness than real power and, at Paneloux's age, a priest had no business to feel that way." The other, a younger man, said that he had had considerable touch with Paneloux of late and had followed the development of his thought. His thinking had evidently become far more radical than he expressed in this sermon, and he intended to set forth, in a pamphlet he was about to publish, that it was illogical for a priest to call a doctor when he was sick.

Shortly after this sermon Paneloux becomes ill. It is uncertain if he has the plague or not; his symptoms are indecisive. Dr. Rieux comes to offer what help he can, but the old priest says: "Thanks. But priests can have no friends, they have given their all to God." (CP, 210) A few hours later he dies and against his name on the index card is recorded—'Doubtful case'. We can be sure that Camus means to infer a second hidden meaning, namely that not only was it uncertain whether the priest had died of the plague but that also, despite his commital of himself to God and rejection of any help man could give him, there had remained for him, underneath all else, a gnawing uncertainty.

Living largely apart from the realities of everyday humdrum life, Paneloux, with the Jesuit's determination and bent towards reason, became an expositor of a theology based upon just retribution. 'An eye for an eye and a tooth for a tooth' is attractive grist for the rational mill. Witnessing the death of M. Othon's son completely undid his confidence in divine justice and rendered void for him his entire former system of theology. Turning to his reason for a solution, he concluded that " his choice would be to believe everything so as not to be forced into denying everything. . . . There was no middle course." The choice lay between accepting what his eyes had seen and hating God, and denying what he had seen, on the basis that man could not comprehend, and loving God. He chose the latter. A strange phenomenon, reason presenting a clear choice and then rationally—although his mind was, without doubt, influenced by what he wanted to believe—recommending the least rational alternative.

I have recounted at some length the development of the thinking of Paneloux for it plays a major part in the quest of Camus. In despair, Paneloux takes the 'leap of faith' into blind belief in God, and is none the happier for it. Camus's exposition of the fallacy of this step and the spiritual position he feels that he him-

self must hold, in order to maintain his moral integrity, are the subject of the next chapter.

10

The Leap of Faith

It is in the *Myth of Sisyphus* that Camus undertakes to examine in detail the leap of faith to which, in despair, Paneloux felt himself driven. "I hold certain facts," he tells us, "from which I cannot separate. What I know, what is certain, what I cannot deny, what I cannot reject—this is what counts. I can negate everything of that part of me that lives on vague nostalgias, except for this desire for unity, this longing to solve, this need for clarity and cohesion. . . .I don't know whether this world has a meaning that transcends it. But I know that I do not know that meaning and that it is impossible for me to know it just now." (CM, 38)

His intellect presents him with certain inalienable truths which he cannot deny, such as the injustice of suffering innocence. In the spiritual side of his nature, not in the realm of the vague nostalgias of his soul, is born a longing for the satisfaction which could only come from a sufficient 'raison d' être' for life as a whole. His reason has shown him the absurd and cornered him in a frustrating impasse. His spirit—recognizing that reason is not everything, nevertheless, in honesty, refusing to categorize it as nothing—gropes for an answer which will encompass the totality of life whilst not doing violence to any aspect of it, reason included.

But the perception of Camus goes beyond this. He knows that he does not possess this meaning which would satisfactorily conclude everything and, indeed, what is more, that it is impossible, with the

faculties available to him, to know it "just now." This does not, however, rule out the possibility of his arriving at such an understanding one day in the future through some medium presently unimaginable to him. The difficulty is to maintain this position whilst waiting for the understanding to come. There are those who tell him that "the intelligence must sacrifice its pride and the reason bow down." To which he replies: "If I recognize the limits of reason, I do not therefore negate it, recognizing its relative powers. I merely want to remain in this middle path where intelligence can remain clear. If that is pride, I see no sufficient reason for giving it up." (CM, 30) It is this middle path which is insufferable to Paneloux; he *has* to have an answer or devise one, and immediately. In the *Myth of Sisyphus* Camus examines a number of different ways in which one and another has sought to justify the leap philosophically and then finally deals at some length with Kierkegaard, who might be called the *leap's* chief exponent.

Karl Jaspers, the existentialist German philosopher, "has found nothing in experience," says Camus, "but the confession of his own impotence. . . . Yet, without justification, he suddenly asserts all at once the transcendent, the essence of experience, and the superhuman significance of life when he writes: 'Does not the failure reveal, beyond any possible explanation and interpretation, not the absence but the existence of transcendence?' . . . . Nothing logical prepares this reasoning. I call it a leap." (CM, 24-5)

Chestov, the Russian philosopher, evidently made the remark: "The only true solution is precisely where human judgment sees no solution. Otherwise, what need would we have of God? We turn toward God only to obtain the impossible. As for the possible, men suffice." Proceeding with this line of thought, Chestov discovers the fundamental absurdity of all existence; but, says Camus, "he does not say—'This is the absurd'—but rather—'This is God: We must rely on Him even if He does not correspond to any of our rational categories.' So that confusion may not be possible, the Russian philosopher hints that this God is perhaps full of hatred, incomprehensible and contradictory; but the more hideous His face, the more he asserts his power. His greatness is his incoherence. His proof is His inhumanity. One must spring into Him and, by this leap, free oneself from rational illusions." (CM, 25-6)

As to the Jesuits, the followers of Ignatius Loyola, they were

required to make the "third sacrifice, namely the sacrifice of the intellect." (CM, 28) There is not much to say about them as it is simply a law of their society. Loyola was an army general before his conversion and he transferred his military mindedness from the battlefield to the realm of spiritual things. If soldiers could be ordered to do this or that and did not have the right to question the validity of the command, then the religious order which he founded could be likewise disciplined to cleave to certain doctrines and reject others without the members having the right to question.

Concerning the mystics, Camus shows profound insight. "To begin with," he says, "The mystics find freedom in giving them-selves. By losing themselves in their God, by accepting His rules, they become secretly free. In spontaneously accepted slavery they recover a deeper independence. But what does that freedom mean? It may be said, above all, that they 'feel' free with regard to them-selves, and not so much free as liberated." (CM, 43) The Jesuits accept a set of rules imposed by a leader on a society and thus, by their leap, are freed from problems their intellect might raise opposing their subordinating themselves to that society. The mystics accept, not man's rules, but God's, and in this acceptance, or leap, have the impression of being free not only from the world but from man and his societies also.

It is with Kierkegaard that Camus deals the most fully for "of all perhaps the most engaging, he—Kierkegaard—for a part of his existence at least does more than discover the absurd, he lives it." (CM,19) The whole subject is not just academic with him: "he wants to be cured. To be cured is his frenzied wish, and it runs through his whole journal. The entire effort of his intelligence is to escape the antinomy of the human condition. An all the more desperate effort since he intermittently perceives its vanity when he speaks of himself, as if neither fear of God nor piety were capable of bringing him peace." (CM, 29) His problem is that, having seen the absurdity of life and this absurdity having awakened in his spirit the nostalgia of the absurd, he does not maintain the equilibrium between the two. "He wants to save himself from that desperate nostalgia that seems to him sterile and void of impli-cation." Unable to bear this nostalgia, fearful as to where it might lead him, Kierkegaard makes his leap to escape it. "If he substitutes for his cry of revolt a frantic adherence [to God by faith], at once

he is led to blind himself to the absurd which hitherto enlightened him and to deify the only certainty he henceforth possesses, the irrational. . . . Thus it is that through a strained subterfuge he he gives the irrational the appearance and God the attributes of the absurd: unjust, incoherent, and incomprehensible." (CM, 28-9) Camus will not do this himself; he refuses either to sell out to his reason or to take a blind leap of faith. Even if he does not have access to the key which would resolve the problem "just now," that is no sufficient reason for him to abandon his position "in this middle of the path where the intelligence can remain clear." The leap of faith would be the coward's way out. "The danger," he says, "lies in the subtle instant that precedes the leap. Being able to remain on that dizzying crest—that is integrity and the rest is sub-terfuge." (CM, 37)

But what of this leap of faith? Is it a Christian concept? Can Kierkegaard justify his position with regard to it? These questions may not seem to be in the direct line of the spiritual quest of Camus but they do relate to it in the long run as examination of them throws light also on Camus's own position in the middle of the path, refusing to be driven to precipitate action either by his reason or the nostalgia of the absurd.

Throughout the Scriptures, the most prominent symbol of the life of faith is Abraham. It is quite natural, therefore, that Kierke-gaard should have chosen his life to be the subject of a major work, *Fear and Trembling,* which was intended to advocate the leap of faith and explore its significance and effects. Kierkegaard uses the Scriptures as they are as the basis for his study, even if he does em-bellish somewhat the accounts in them by his vivid imagination; thus we can meet him on this ground and test by the Scriptures what he says.

"By faith Abraham went out from the land of his fathers," he tells us, "and became a sojourner in the land of promise. He left one thing behind, took one thing with him: He left his earthly understanding behind and took his faith with him." (KF, 31) This looks harmless enough on the surface, but is it true? If it is true, then Abraham took a leap of faith and renounced his earthly understanding. There is no evidence, however, that Abraham was ever conscious of making such a renunciation. There is further light on this whole incident, not in the Old Testament but in the New,

when, in the opening words of his speech before the council at Jerusalem, Stephen said: "The God of Glory appeared unto our father Abraham, when he was in Mesopotamia, before he dwelt in Haran, and said unto him—'Get thee out of thy land, and from thy kindred and come unto the land that I will shew thee" (*Acts*, 7.2-3) Thus, according to Stephen, before there was any movement by faith, there was a direct revelation from God, and 'The God of Glory' at that! What was that revelation like? How can we conjecture? But we do know, from the record, that later in his life God appeared on other occasions to Abraham as in the 17th chapter of Genesis when He appeared to him and said "I am El Shaddai"; or again, in the 18th chapter, "The Lord appeared unto him by the oaks of Mamre . . . and he lifted up his eyes and looked and lo, three men stood over against him; and when he saw them . . . he said—'My Lord.' The first appearance was without doubt the most awe-inspiring of all as it was the 'God of Glory'. Now, whilst it would be idle to try to conjure up a picture in our minds of such a visitation, yet it is most important that we grasp the significance of it. Abraham was a young man living in Mesopotamia knowing only the idolatry which was the religion of his 'land' and his 'kindred'. This visitation, wholly unanticipated, provided sufficient impetus to start him going along a road, hitherto untrod, toward "the land which I will shew thee." Thus revelation came first and the movement by faith came second, in the light of the revelation.

Now Kierkegaard affirms that Abraham left his earthly wisdom behind him. If this were the case then the effect of catching a glimpse of God would be to cause man to negate his reason and reckon it to be untrustworthy. But there is no evidence that this was ever the case either with Abraham or with any other character in the Bible. The effect is rather the reverse. Abraham's receiving a revelation from God can be compared to a blind man's receiving his sight. Before he could see, he had to feel his way around as best he could, guided by the touch of his fingers. On receiving his sight, his reaction would not be that he could now dispense with his fingers but rather that he could guide them and use them always to profit, the sight delivering them from their fumbling of the past. Spiritual revelation, be it of the limited sort described by Camus in the 'Exile and the Kingdom', which is the subject of the next

chapter, or be it of a more ultimate nature, is always liberating and never shackling; it puts reason into its right place and looses it to function properly.

"By faith Abraham, when he was called, obeyed to go out unto a place which he was to receive for an inheritance" (*Hebrews* 11). First there was the revelation of the God of Glory who called Abraham and told him to go out. Then, on the part of Abraham, there was the initial response towards obedience to the call; and finally, by faith, he obeyed and went. But whence the faith? "By Grace have ye been saved through faith, and that not of your-selves: it is the gift of God" (*Ephesians,* 2.8). What agonies theologians have suffered trying to define faith; whether it has its origins in man or God, or how much from the one and how much from the other! Indeed, it is impossible to reconcile rationally what has been said above with the command: "Believe . . . and thou shalt be saved!" which would seem to be designed to evoke a dormant faith in the hearer. This enigma, however, is no more than a variant of the controversy of free will versus predestination which raged between the Jansenists and Jesuits in the 17th Century and which reason is impotent to resolve. Camus says: "I am not a philosopher, I know only how to speak of those things I have experienced." This, I feel sure, would have been Abraham's reply to anyone who had asked him to explain how, if faith was the gift of God and not an attribute of man, he had managed to make any response at all God-ward. Evidently Abraham *saw* the God of Glory and heard His call, his heart responded to *obey,* and faith was given to him to obey and *go.*

Kierkegaard's problem is that he sees Abraham's faith as a strength in himself which he had to foster. "Abraham believed," he says, "and held fast the expectation. If Abraham had wavered, he would have given up." (KF, 32) There is some truth in this but an overall false impression. The reader who is unacquainted with the Scriptures would receive the notion that Abraham was resolute and unflinching and never faltered; and this simply was not the case. The fact is that in almost every major move he did falter and then, as a result of the experience which invariably followed such lapses, he came back to his true ground again and got through.

He was called to "come into the land which I will shew thee"

but he was sidetracked, probably by the influence of his father who felt he had travelled far enough for an old man, and stopped in Haran—"They went forth to go into the land of Canaan and they came unto Haran and dwelt there"; and there they remained until Terah, Abraham's father, died. (*Genesis*, 11.31) Then God spoke again to him and once more "they went forth to go into the land of Canaan", but on this occasion "into the land of Canaan they came!" (*Genesis*, 12.5) No mistake about it this time!

There was a famine in the land, so Abraham did what he should not have done and went down into Egypt and even descended to pretending that his wife was his sister, fearing lest the inhabitants might slay him for her. God had to plague Pharaoh to get him back up to the Promised Land again. He was told he would have a son by Sarah, but, when that avenue seemed barren, in a moment of despair and at the instigation of his wife, he resorted to having a child by Hagar as a substitute. But this was unacceptable to God who, later, gave him Isaac by Sarah at a time when both of them were past the age for it to be humanly possible. If he had always been perfect and had never faltered and there had been faith in him to meet any exigency, then the test described in *Genesis* (chapter 22) where he is called upon to sacrifice his son would have been as Kierkegaard describes it—a fantastic, unbelievable display of sublime confidence in God, superhuman in its being completely undaunted by any barrage reason might launch against it. Actually it was not so much his successes as his failures which strengthened the faith of Abraham. Each time he failed, he discovered that God did not let him go, nor did He alter what He had determined to do, nor the way in which He had determined to do it. Thus the vicissitudes he passed through served not so much to strengthen a faith which was already in himself as to deepen his confidence in the faithfulness of God and make him increasingly wary of his own tendency to compromise and its consequences. Could Abraham read Kierkegaard's *Fear and Trembling,* he would feel sorry for the writer, I think, feeling that he had completely missed the point.

In contradistinction to Kierkegaard's interpretation of the episode recounted in *Genesis* (Chapter 22), where Abraham is called on to sacrifice his son, I would briefly here suggest what would seem to be nearer the facts:

As Abraham entered the twilight of old age, God wanted to know just how much he had learned of Him and His faithfulness during his long and tortuous voyage through life. Could He now count on him as a friend? Was the moral ground at long last established in this man's life to justify his being chosen to become the father of a people who would be peculiarly God's in the earth? So God decided to prove Abraham and spoke directly to him: "Take thy son, thine only son whom thou lovest . . . and offer him for a burnt offering." What could be harder to accept? Yet here he was nearing the end of life and, if one lesson stood out above all others as he looked back across the years, it was that, every time he had obeyed, it had brought blessing and, every time he had faltered and adopted a compromise course, it had resulted in confusion. He dared not, at this crucial juncture, disobey. Isaac represented the very way by which God was to fulfil the promise of seed as the sand and the stars for multitude—he was the very embodiment of the hope of fulfilment for Abraham; but he had been given miraculously, contrary to nature, by God; and Abraham dared not disobey. Thus he went forward, not without inward apprehensions, for sure, yet knowing from experience that any other course would lead to sorrow. At the last moment God provided a sacrifice, a ram caught in a thicket. Then God said to him: "In blessing I will bless thee . . . because thou hast obeyed my voice."

Here again it was a direct speaking, a voice, and the issue was obedience. There is no leap of faith—Camus's attitude to this matter is much more in accord with Scriptural principle than Kierkegaard's. Kierkegaard is like the man who builds on sand, who is so anxious to see the house go up that he will not take time with the foundation; indeed, he is frightened of what he might unearth if he started digging. The leap-of-faith man has no other foundation than his own initiative and determination to make that leap, and he is always plagued by intellectual problems afterwards.

But was this the way in which things functioned in the Old Testament and is there a different modus operandi in the New? To answer this question it seems appropriate to examine briefly the spiritual beginnings of the two principal personages of the pre-resurrection and post-pentecostal eras, Peter and Paul, respectively.

After walking with His disciples for perhaps more than two of

the three years that He spent with them, and increasingly conscious of what lay ahead for Him in Jerusalem of sufferings and for them of trials, Jesus Christ must have been deeply preoccupied as to how much they had really understood when one day He asked: "Who do men say that the Son of man is?" (*Matthew*, 16.13) Was He a little apprehensive about putting the question directly to them and thus led up to it gently by enquiring about others first? After all, everything hung on their position spiritually and, if nothing had been wrought in them inwardly, the impending experiences at Jerusalem would be disastrous. "Some say John the Baptist; some Elijah: and others Jeremiah, or one of the prophets," they replied. Then, taking the bull by the horns: "But who say ye that I am?" to which Simon Peter answered: "Thou art the Christ, the Son of the living God!" "Blessed art thou Simon Bar-Jonah," said Jesus, "for flesh and blood hath not revealed it unto thee, but my father which is in Heaven."

There are two most interesting elements in this; first, that He, as a man, could not transmit this revelation to Peter, He had to wait for the Father to do it and, secondly, He made no mention of faith; He simply said that Peter was fortunate or happy that this revelation had been vouchsafed to him. He goes on to say: "Thou art Petros (Greek for a little rock) and upon this Petra (Greek for a massive cliff or boulder) I will build My church." Everything for Kierkegaard is built upon the leap of faith which has no more behind it foundationally than his own initiative and determination. For Peter it was altogether different, a revelation had been given into him which was a Petra, massive cliff or boulder, upon which something solid and lasting could be built, and he himself became a little rock or stone in consequence; the first of the living stones of which the House of God was to be constructed.

The order of experience is just the same for the apostle Paul who was on his way from Jerusalem to Damascus to persecute the Christians there with the express purpose of stamping out this new movement before it really got started. On his way "suddenly there shone round about him a light out of heaven . . . and he heard a voice." (*Acts*, 9.3-4) Later, describing this incident to King Agrippa, he said: "Wherefore, O King Agrippa, I was not disobedient to the heavenly vision." (*Acts*, 26.19) There was a vision or revelation, and the immediate issue for Paul was obedience. It could be argued,

of course, that he was a special case and he was; but so is everyone, in measure. There is no evidence that anyone in the New Testament became a Christian without there having first dawned upon that one an understanding as to who Jesus Christ is; that understanding never came after and as a consequence of a leap of faith. It seems that, Scripturally, the order is a constant for all times, Old Testament and New—Revelation, then the response to obey and, finally, the receipt of faith for movement.

The question naturally arises as to why some receive revelation in these matters and others do not and as to whether there is something arbitrary about this. This will be touched upon in the last chapter after we have studied Camus's understanding of revelation in the chapter to come.

I I

Revelation

Even the student who engaged in the most cursory study of the life
and work of Saint Augustine could not fail to be impressed by the
dramatic experience which, at about the age of thirty-two, revolu-
tionized his life and launched him upon his ministry. It was no
cursory study of this author, however, which terminated in Camus's
writing his M.A. thesis about his work; he must have read Augustine's own account of this spiritual crisis in his "Confessions" and
pondered the matter. A comparison between the experience and
works of Augustine on the one hand and those of Thomas Aquinas
on the other emphasizes even more the significance of this crisis;
the former having received his revelation at the outset of his
ministry and the latter at the conclusion of his. Late in life when,
after receiving a profound spiritual revelation, Thomas Aquinas
was urged by a friend to finish his almost completed *Summa Theo-
logica,* which he had purposed to be an exhaustive encyclopedia of
Christian theology, he evidently replied: "Such secrets have been
revealed to me that all I have written now appears to be of little
worth." Herein lies the explanation for the substantial difference
in tone between these two authors. Whereas there is a ring of
authority about Augustine as, with the Scripture for his basis, he
makes authoritative pronouncements; Aquinas appeals much to the
words of others, particularly Augustine, and then deduces through
his reason.

The profligate life he had led, a deep sense of inability to master lust, and a godly patient mother combined to drive Augustine to the conviction that, if he was ever to be cured, it would be as a result of some assistance which would have to come from outside himself. He wanted to serve God and yet felt hopelessly unable to lead the continent life required of the priesthood. He addressed himself to take the leap of faith, but honest recognition of his real condition withheld him. "I stood on the brink of resolution," he says, "waiting to take fresh breath. I tried again and came a little nearer my goal, and then a little nearer still, so that I could almost reach out and grasp it. But I did not reach it. I could not reach out to it or grasp it, because I held back from the step by which I should die to death and become alive to life. My lower instincts, which had taken firm hold of me, were stronger than the higher, which were untried. And the closer I came to the moment which was to mark the great change in me, the more I shrank from it in horror. But it did not drive me back or turn me from my purpose: it merely left me hanging in suspense." (SC, 175) This is surely quite similar to the position Camus describes and which he calls the only integrity, ". . . This middle of the path where the intelligence can remain clear." (CM, 30) Camus arrived at this position by discovering his inability to solve the intellectual and spiritual enigma of the meaning of life and, moreover, that such a solution was impossible to him "just now." Augustine arrived at the same impasse but by a different route—the discovery of his inability to harness the lusts of his flesh. The leap of faith is, of course, a more tempting avenue of escape to the one who has a mental rather than a physical impasse to negotiate. The man plagued by the physical knows in advance that, should he take the leap, he would be unable to avoid tangible evidence as to its efficacy. Indeed, he may try it but, if he is moderately honest with himself, will have to admit its impotence. He may, of course, like those whom Clamence despises, say to himself that he "is not a very pretty sight, that's certain! Well, we won't go into the details! We'll just liquidate it all at once on the cross!" and thereby make a leap and a sidestep all in one! (CF, 114) The leap to appease the intellect God-ward and the side-step to evade the issue of his actual moral condition.

In the intellectual and spiritual realms, Camus was too honest to

let himself be fooled into a false peace which the leap might give; he prized his integrity too much. Augustine was the same in the physical and spiritual; he refused to pretend to himself that he had found any solution until some radical change, of which he was incapable, delivered him from being the slave of his lusts. We will let him recount, in his own words, the sequence of events which led to this crisis: "I felt I was still the captive of my sins, and in my misery I kept crying 'How long shall I go on saying "To-morrow, to-morrow?" Why not now? Why not make an end of my ugly sins at this moment?' I was asking myself these question, weeping all the while with the most bitter sorrow in my heart, when all at once I heard the sing-song voice of a child in a nearby house. Whether it was the voice of a boy or a girl I cannot say, but again and again it repeated the refrain—'Take it and read, take it and read!' At this I looked up, thinking hard whether there was any kind of game in which children used to chant words like these, but I could not remember ever hearing them before. I stemmed my flood of tears and stood up, telling myself that this could only be a divine command to open up my book of Scripture and read the first passage upon which my eyes should fall. For I had heard the story of Antony, and I remembered how he had happened to go into a church while the gospel was being read and had taken it as a counsel addressed to himself when he heard the words—'Go home and sell all that belongs to you. Give to the poor, and so the treasure you shall have shall be in heaven; then come back and follow me.' By this divine pronouncement he had been converted. . . . So I hurried back to the place where Alypius was sitting, for when I stood up to move away I had put down the book containing Paul's epistles. I seized it and opened it, and in silence I read the first passage on which my eyes fell: "Not in revelling and drunkenness, not in lust and wantonness, not in quarrels and rivalries. Rather, arm yourselves with the Lord Jesus Christ; spend no more thought on nature and nature's appetites." I had no wish to read more and no need to do so. For in an instant, as I came to the end of the sentence, it was as though the light of confidence flooded into my heart and all the darkness of doubt was dispelled. . . . My looks were quite calm as I told Alypius what had happened to me." (SC, 177)

But revelation is not confined to one all-inclusive realisation. Any

experience in which the spiritual understanding is enlightened is of the same nature and carries with it a certainty and authority. Camus's books are full of incidents where truths as to the nature of man and life dawn upon the characters; it is in the group of short stories entitled *The Exile and the Kingdom,* however, that he undertakes specifically to examine this principle and its operation as far as he had experience of it. The title embodies the whole concept. For a number of reasons man finds himself in exile from society, shut in on himself and limited in his participation with others and his usefulness to them. He needs a revelation, the dawning of an understanding to break upon him, in order that he may be freed into this sharing with others; and, sometimes, this is not accomplished without a period of deeper exile as in the case of Jonas. But to what extent are the revelations that these characters receive efficacious; do they represent something which will prove to be at least mildly revolutionary in effect and of lasting significance?

Janine of *The Adulterous Wife* is approaching middle age. She had married Marcel at least partly for fear of being left alone later in life. There were no children and Marcel, who had been quite an interesting and considerate husband to her when they were first married, became more and more preoccupied with his business and seemingly insensitive towards her. They take a business trip together, south from the Mediterranean coast, to the small towns where Marcel will seek to sell his fabrics. Everything in the climate, landscape, and expression of the people seems to present a hostile front to Janine and to emphasize her confinement and limitation tied to Marcel. They go together to see the view from the high wall surrounding the town they are visiting and look out across the vast open expanse of the desert. Later, during the night when her husband is asleep, Janine slips from the bedroom and returns alone to this wall where, contemplating the stars adrift in the sky, "she opened herself a little more to the night. After so many years of fleeing from fear . . . she was finally coming to a halt. At the same time it seemed as if she was finding her roots. . . . The waters of the night began to fill Janine and, drowning the cold, arose little by little from the hidden depths of her being to overflow in uninterrupted waves up to her mouth filled with groans. The very next moment, the entire sky extended itself above her, face downwards

towards the earth." (CT, 1572) She quietly returns to the hotel and to bed with her husband who, waking and seeing her tears, asks what is the matter. "It's nothing, my dear, it's nothing!" she replies, knowing he would be unable to understand "just now!" (CT, 198)

This is similar to the experience of Meursault when, after his outburst with the prison chaplain, he meditates on his lot: "It was as if that great rush of anger had washed me clean, emptied me of hope, and, gazing up at the dark sky spangled with its signs and stars, for the first time, I laid my heart open to the benign indifference of the universe. To feel it so like myself, indeed, so brotherly, made me realize that I'd been happy, and that I was happy still"— a dawning or realization which mollified an impasse and made it tolerable. (CS, 154) Janine was metaphorically adulterous in her association with the stars and night, separate from her husband. Naturally one hopes that, being herself freed by the discovery she had made, she would be able to return to her old confining circumstances, live above them and, maybe, help others—even Marcel; as the drowning man, if it were suddenly to dawn on him how to swim, could use the element which was drowning him, water, to help him to get somewhere.

Yvars of *The Silent Ones* shares the lot of a small group of workers in a barrel factory who had been on strike for higher wages. The strike had failed; barrel making was a dying industry and the young owner, however much he would have liked to help, was financially incapable of making any concessions to his workers. Most of them, Yvars included, show their discontent the first day back by sulkily refusing to speak to him. During the day there is an emergency; the owner's daughter falls sick and is taken away in an ambulance. Yvars and others would have liked to say something comforting to the father but they discover that their sulky behavior of the morning paralyzes them and morally disqualifies them from uttering a word. They had sought to make the owner suffer by ostracizing him and now, when they would like to communicate, they come up against a hidden law which impedes them. Of course, they could have overcome the impasse on the spot by swallowing their pride and apologizing for their earlier behavior; but, as they were unwilling to humble themselves, only time could thaw the frigidity of the atmosphere. There was a lesson for Yvars in all

of this but, unhappily, he only half-learnt it. In the evening, to ease his conscience and bolster his pride of position in his home as a kind of retribution for having lost it at work, he said to his wife concerning the factory owner: "It was all his fault!" (CT, 1606) This naturally was insufficient to give him the release and escape he inwardly craved, so he added he wished they were young again so that they could cross the sea and start afresh on a new life.

Daru of *The Guest* had been isolated by the snow in his hilltop school for some days when Balducci, the gendarme, arrived with an Arab who was being held for murder. The gendarme had orders to leave the Arab with Daru, who was to take him on to the prison the following day. Daru refused to accept the charge but the gendarme, feeling free from any further responsibility in the matter himself, left the Arab and departed. Try as he might, Daru could not bring himself to accept the Arab's presence and thus was unable to fall asleep closeted with him in the same room. During the night the Arab rose and crept stealthily to the door; Daru was glad and hoped he was going to escape, but it was soon evident that the Arab had just gone out to relieve himself for he came quietly back in again and lay down. The obvious confidence that the Arab had in him and his quiet resignation and acceptance of his circumstances liberated Daru, at one stroke, from all his anger and hostility. He rolled over and fell asleep at once. His discovery is similar, in measure, to that of Yvars, namely that hostilities have a boomerang effect, robbing the one who has them of his peace and liberty to function in relation to others. The following day, Daru gave the Arab food and money and the option of going alone to the prison or South to join a nomadic tribe who would accept him and give him refuge. The Arab chose prison, fearful of the uncertainty and unfamiliar territory the other course might lead him into. The end is tragic as Daru is misunderstood by the Arabs who think he has delivered the wanted man, their brother, to prison, and by the French who know, through the gendarme, that he refused to fulfill the orders!

Of the remaining three stories, all of which deal more directly with spiritual matters, *The Stone which Grows* has already been examined in some detail in our chapter 7. D'Arrast felt himself apart and exiled from society until, after carrying the stone to Le Coq's house, he was accepted by the native population of the

poor quarter of the town. The practical question naturally arises as to where he went from there! He could hardly settle down and live with those who had accepted him without abandoning his own countrymen and his occupation. But the experience had been a salutary one for him and especially for Le Coq also, whom he had helped to liberate spiritually. Perhaps there was a lasting effect in his learning to reach out to others rather than hanging back, semi-tongue-tied, waiting for others to approach him.

The Renegade tells of a young enthusiastic catholic missionary, driven by a lust for power, sallying forth, against the counsel of his elders, to the most difficult territory, a salt-mining town in North Africa inhabited by evil, vicious, fetish-worshipping natives. His ambition, quite unconsciously no doubt, was to dominate these people by converting them spiritually to his religion. The reverse takes place, they dominate him by employing the very same tactics as he, but in the physical realm, driving him by brute force to submit to their fetish. Systematically they break him down until, with them, he worships hate. Another and older missionary is sent out to replace him whom he waylays and shoots. The old man smiles at him as he dies; but the renegade, unable to bear it, smashes his face with the butt of his rifle to eradicate the smile— and to his amazement he finds himself weeping. His masters, fearful that he will bring the wrath of the Europeans upon them for killing the old man, beat him and lash him to a saddle as if crucified and are about to leave him to die in the desert when he hears a voice which says: "If you consent to die for hatred and power, who will pardon us?" (CT, 1591) He pleads with his tormentors that the city of mercy be built where there was a city of hate but, in a final gesture as they leave, one of their number crams his mouth with a handful of salt. Quite a similar situation to the stoning of Stephen at which Saul, later to become Paul, officiated. His words of forgiveness and face which became as "the face of an angel" must have haunted Saul, driving him deeper into his "threatenings and slaughter" (*Acts, 9.1*) until he met his spiritual Waterloo. This is the one occasion in the works of Camus where building a city of mercy is mentioned, and grace, if not expressly spelled out, is at least indicated in the old missionary's smile.

Jonas, partly autobiographical of Camus's experience in Paris after World War II when he came quickly into wide acclaim as

an author, is a clear allusion, particularly with its three days and nights of solitude, to the Biblical Jonah. This latter, when ordered of God to proceed East to Nineveh to warn the Ninevites of impending judgment if they did not repent, went rather in the opposite direction and sought a ship going West to Tarshish. A storm arose and, at his request, the seamen threw Jonah overboard, whereupon a fish swallowed him and dived to the sea bottom. "The deep was round about me, the weeds were wrapped about my head" said Jonah. "When my soul fainted within me, I remembered the Lord. . . . They that regard lying vanities forsake their own mercy." (*Jonah*, 2) What drove him first to disobedience and thence to this awful experience? The Ninevites had repeatedly overrun the Jews and ravaged their land, incurring their hate. Jonah knew that if he went and called them to repent they would do so and God, being a God of mercy, would pardon them. He felt so bitter towards them that he preferred to "forsake his own mercy" if this would mean that they would be punished. The three days and nights brought him to his senses and, in measure, enlarged him. First he had been exiled by his hatred; the three days and nights of forced exile brought to him a revelation of his condition. When given the second opportunity to go and preach to Nineveh, he went but, afterwards, sat on a hill nearby and sulked waiting to see what would transpire. He did not fully experience the deliverance of a wholly enlarged soul until God enquired of him: "Should I not have pity on Nineveh, the great city wherein are more than six score thousand persons that cannot discern between their right hand and their left hand; and also much cattle?"

Camus's Jonas experiences sudden success as a painter. His admirers fill his time and put him off his painting, for which he loses his flair. The critics notice his decline and speak of it and, to avoid them, he begins to frequent taverns in a section of town where he is unknown. He is unfaithful to his wife, whom he leaves largely alone in the apartment with the two children. Touched by the kindness of his friend, Rateau, and the obvious suffering of his wife, he begins to come to his senses. Having purchased some lumber, he builds a little platform for himself, high up at the end of the apartment's dark corridor and here he sits alone for three days and nights in meditation. At the end of this period, the others find a canvas on which he has just written one word of which one

letter is indistinguishable; it is either 'Solitaire' or 'Solidaire.' Camus's meaning is clearly that, in order to be 'solidaire'— in solid friendly communication with others—it is necessary first to be 'solitaire.'

Jonas is very like Jonah. He allows his resentment of the critics to drive him from his friends and home, and even to "forsake his own mercy." The loyalty and affection of Rateau and his wife touch him and, finally, after the three days and nights, the stupidity of the suffering he was bringing on himself and others dawns on him. With Jonah the problem is deeper and far more radical—he was obsessed with justice and wanted the Ninevites to get what they richly deserved. He knew that God, being a God of mercy, would pardon them and let them off free, and he just couldn't bear the thought. He needed, not just to see his stupidity, as did Jonas, but to experience an inward enlarging and change of attitude whereby, contrary to nature, he would wish for mercy and forgiveness to be bestowed upon those who did not deserve it.

At first *The Fall* was intended to be the seventh of these short stories but, in the writing, it outgrew the others and became a book on its own, containing the most comprehensive revelation of the nature of man and the misery he experiences as the victim of his pride.

But what can be said of the revelations contained both in *The Fall* and in the stories of *The Exile and the Kingdom?* What is revealed and how substantial will the effect be as to a change of character or outlook? In most cases, the dawning is no more than a deeper understanding of the nature of man himself and the spiritual or psychological laws which govern his being either shut up in himself or released into free communication with others. Meursault and Janine do go a little beyond this in experiencing some sort of merging with the universe which frees them, probably by their receiving an enlarged understanding of their relative insignificance and thus the smallness of their problems. The vastness of the universe seems to release them to a resignation which, as Saint-Exupéry discovered, leads to peace. Jonas, too, though he lost the conscious presence of his guiding star during his period of dissolution, found it again after the three days and nights on his little platform. But what these celestial images are supposed to imply is not clear.

Camus expresses the truths of man and of his condition; there is no case in which an all-inclusive *truth* is even hinted at for it is, indeed, the Kingdom of men and not of God with which he has to do. It is therefore at this juncture that this book necessarily changes tone; for hitherto Camus has been leading us, he has opened the door to every avenue of study we have pursued, but this was as far as he went. "In psychology as in logic, there are truths but not truth," he says, and the same applies to his work. (CM,15) He knew that there must be a *truth* of man, for man required it; but he also knew that he did not know it. Indeed, the older he got, the further he apparently felt he was from it. In his latter years he said: "What is man worth? What is man? All my life after what I have seen, I shall remain profoundly mistrustful and perplexed about him." Madame Jacqueline Bernard, who worked with him in the resistance newspaper *Combat* during World War II, confided to the author that, towards the end of his life, even though he had become wealthy from the royalties on his books, Camus seemed none the happier. It is recorded that he found an increasing need for solitude and tended to spend more time on his own. Some attribute this desire to the Spanish side of his nature inherited from his mother. There is, I think, another explanation—at least in part. If "the *truth* shall make you free" (*John*, 8.23), truths, although some of them may assist in negotiating some hazards and pitfalls encountered in relationships, will for the most part weigh down and depress the one who sees them. For instance, Clamence did not really find a solution to what he had seen; it was as if human nature was stripped naked before him and he saw pride in all its ugliness; such a seeing does not make life any easier to live, rather the contrary. My interpretation of the conclusion of *The Adulterous Wife* may well have been considerably more optimistic than Camus ever intended. After returning from her nocturnal trip to the wall surrounding the city, Janine slips into bed again. Marcel is disturbed and gets up to take a drink of water as if something as simple as that satisfied his pedestrian soul whereas it took the whole universe with all its stars to assuage hers: "he was just about to slip back under the sheets when, with one knee on the bed, he looked at her blankly. She was weeping unrestrainedly and uncontrollably. 'It's nothing, my dear', she said; 'It's nothing!'" (CT, 1573) I said it was to be hoped that she could now live above her

situation, but quite the opposite is all too possible. What she had seen might well have accentuated the limitations and confinement of her circumstances. After all it was the truths he had seen and the conscious lack of the *truth* he could not attain which drove Caligula to become what he became and do what he did. It is frequently not ignorance of man's plight but consciousness of it and the inability to find an adequate solution which drives to insanity. "A man is always prey to his truths," writes Camus in *The Myth of Sisyphus.* "Once he has admitted them, he cannot free himself from them. One has to pay something."

The stories of *The Exile and the Kingdom* are delightful reading, and some have a mystical quality about them, yet they evoke an inevitable sadness and a sense of lack of fulfilment in face of the down-to-earth practical question: "Yes, but what then?" In talking with the author about the tragedy of Camus's early death, a well-known English critic of French literature made the comment that he and his colleagues felt there was so much more to come from Camus's pen had he lived. Was there any more left to be said without his first having arrived, by revelation, at something which would adequately satisfy "this longing to solve, this need for clarity and cohesion"? Others have said of him that in two novels, two or three plays, and two philosophical essays he encompassed the entire plight of mid-20th century man. We arrive with him at that point which precedes the leap of faith, the place which he says is alone "integrity, and all the rest—subterfuge." It is truly, as he says, "a dizzying crest"; (CM, 37) and all there was to be said of the road which leads to it, he had expressed.

I 2

Justice and Grace

Of all the works of Camus, *The Plague* leaves the reader with the loftiest sense of the dignity of man and his resilience in the face of adversity. Camus probably spent more time in the preparation of this book than any other and poured into it not just a depiction of the weaknesses and frailties of human nature but a portrayal of what the 'good man' should be like, the man after Camus's heart. The full abilities of a tennis player will never be displayed until he is matched against another as good as he; likewise it takes another man of similar outlook to draw out, in dialogue, the deepest thoughts and concerns of a serious man of measure. Thus a Tarrou was necessary to bring to light all the wisdom and values inherent in a Dr. Rieux and vice versa. This is not all, however, for there is a distinction between these two. Whereas Tarrou aspired to be a 'Saint', that is, to arrive at a certain inner state of peace, the ambition of Dr. Rieux was to be a 'man', to live in relation to others in a way which would be meaningful and, in helping them, to find fulfilment. They each represent one half of Camus's ideal man, Tarrou the meditative, spiritual side and Dr. Rieux the practical, down-to-earth doctor who finds his raison d'être in service.

These two are most appealing; they embody just about all a serious-minded, purposeful person could wish a man to be. There is, however, one note struck, particularly by Tarrou, which is insistently sad and rings as a kind of death knell throughout the book.

He and Dr. Rieux had been talking together at length about human suffering and God; finally Tarrou says: "Now I can picture what this plague means to you" and the Doctor replies: "Yes, a never ending defeat." A little later Tarrou takes up the conversation where it was left off: "you are perfectly right" he says, and the doctor asks him: "but you, what do you know about it?" to which he replies: "Ah! I've little left to learn."—"Do you really imagine that you know everything about life?" The answer came in the same cool, confident tone: "Yes!" (CP, 118-19)

Later in the book when the battle against the plague is almost won, the two go out onto a terrace one evening and Tarrou recounts his life story, and the same wistfully sad note is struck. After having expounded to Dr. Rieux his understanding of the spiritual plague, Tarrou concludes: "Yes, it's a wearying business being plague-stricken. But it's still more wearying to refuse to be it. That's why everybody in the world looks so tired; everyone is more or less sick with the plague. But that is also why some of us, those who want to get the plague out of their systems, feel such a desperate weariness, a weariness from which nothing remains to set us free except death." (CP, 229) Tarrou felt he knew all there was to know and that he was caught in a spiritual trap from which there was no possible escape during his lifetime. A fatalistic hopelessness which is made the sadder by his selflessness. One does not grieve so much when a person's reaction to this plight is: "Let's eat drink and be merry for tomorrow we shall die"; but that outlook finds no place in the thought of Tarrou and Rieux who, though knowingly up against impossible odds, yet give themselves unstintingly for the benefit of others. But even their giving is affected by their outlook; it is not that they are unsympathetic; yet a sombre seriousness, born of a lack of hope, is ever present. Whence this pessimistic, though controlled, despair?

The distinction between spiritual things and religious has already been made in our chapter 7, "Spiritual Revolt." Camus renounced religion; according to Roger Quilliot he regarded it as "either an old ladies' occupation, something to keep them busy while awaiting death, or the vague expression of the aspirations of youth towards something larger than itself, the obscure desire to survive and to give a meaning to life." (CE, 1220) But he goes further and renounces essential Christianity, focusing on the doctrine of the

atonement as justification for the position he adopts. "In its essence, Christianity (and this is its paradoxical greatness) is a doctrine of injustice. It is founded upon the sacrifice of the innocent and the acceptance of this sacrifice." (CE, 271) To quote Thomas Hanna on the subject: "This is to say that, to Camus's mind, Jesus of Nazareth was an innocent man unjustly killed; from no point of view can he rule out the fact of the injustice in this event. Hence, when Christians, viewing this event, accept it as a sacrifice—that is, when they accept it as right and necessary—they have denied the one undeniable truth in this event, which is that it is horrible and unjust that an innocent man should be killed." (BV, 49) It follows inexorably that, if Camus renounced Christianity and could not accept the death of Christ on account of the injustice of innocence suffering for the guilty, then the absolute, the lodestar which formed the basis for this judgment, was Justice.

"From the moment that man submits God to moral judgment" says Camus in *The Rebel* "he kills Him in his own heart. And then what is the basis of morality? God is denied in the name of Justice." (CR, 62) The rebel, says Camus, "opposes the principle of justice which he finds in himself to the principle of injustice which he sees being applied in the world. . . . He defies more than he denies. Originally, at least, he does not suppress God: he merely talks to Him as an equal. But it is not a polite dialogue. It is a polemic animated by the desire to conquer. The slave begins by demanding justice and ends by wanting to wear a crown. . . . When the throne of God is overturned, the rebel realizes that it is now his own responsibility to create the justice, order, and unity that he sought in vain within his own condition, and in this way to justify the fall of God." (CR, 25) It almost seems that Camus has been snared by the cry of Prometheus and then adopted it: "Oh justice! Oh, my mother!" He concludes, a touch sardonically: "In one sense, Christianity's bitter intuition and legitimate pessimism concerning human behavior is based on the assumption that overall injustice is as satisfying to man as total justice. Only the sacrifice of an innocent God could justify the endless and universal torture of innocence. Only the most abject suffering by God could assuage man's agony. If everything, without exception, in heaven and earth is doomed to pain and suffering, then a strange form of happiness is possible." (CR, 34)

In considering the novel, *the Plague,* as a whole, it is obvious that the focus of the entire work is on the night when the son of M. Othon dies of the disease. This scene is unusually dramatized and, after the death, Dr. Rieux, for the only time in the entire book, loses his temper. "Rieux was already on his way out, walking so quickly and with such a strange look on his face that Paneloux put out an arm to check him when he was about to pass him in the doorway. 'Come Doctor', he began. Rieux swung round on him fiercely 'Ah! That child was innocent and you know it as well as I do!' He strode on, brushing past Paneloux, and walked across the school playground. Sitting on a wooden bench under the dingy, stunted trees, he wiped off the sweat that was beginning to run into his eyes. He felt like shouting imprecations—anything to loosen the stranglehold lashing his heart with steel. Heat was flooding down between the branches of the fig tree. A white haze spreading rapidly over the blue of the morning sky made the air yet more stifling. Rieux lay back wearily on the bench. . . . He heard a voice behind him: 'Why was that anger in your voice just now? What we'd been seeing was as unbearable to me as it was to you.' Rieux turned towards Paneloux: 'I know. I'm sorry. But weariness is a kind of madness. And there are times when the only feeling I have is one of mad revolt.' 'I understand', Paneloux said in a low voice. 'That sort of thing is revolting because it passes our human understanding. But perhaps we should love what we cannot understand.' Rieux straightened up slowly. He gazed at Paneloux, summoning to his gaze all the strength and fervor he could muster against his weariness. Then he shook his head. 'No, Father. I've a very different idea of love. And until my dying day I shall refuse to love a scheme of things in which children are put to torture'." (CP, 196)

It is no exaggeration, I believe, to say that Camus was obsessed with the idea of justice; and it is impossible to hold such an obsession without becoming simultaneously blinded to grace. It is indeed a flash of honesty when, in the very same conversation a few moments later, after Paneloux said "I've just realized what is meant by grace," Rieux replied more gently: "It's something I haven't got; that I know. But I'd rather not discuss that with you." (CP, 197) This is surely not only a confession of conscious lack on the part of Rieux, but a veiled admission by his creator also; an admission that such a thing as grace perhaps existed but he had no experience of it.

Here, I cannot refrain from sharing a delightful little parabolic illustration of the distinction between Justice and Grace. It was told to me by an American Negro who was studying at Oxford University at the time. There was a boys' private school in the States, he said, and in it one black boy and all the rest white. The faculty were all white and bent on maintaining white supremacy. In athletics, when it came to the high jump, the faculty, imagining no one noticed what they were doing, lowered the bar a little when the white boys were jumping and raised it a little for the black boy. The boys, all of them, black and white, saw what was going on and reacted accordingly. The white boys relaxed, knowing they only had to make a four foot ten effort to clear five feet, whereas the black boy braced himself seeing a five foot two inch effort would be needed for him to clear the same height. My friend ended the story by turning to me and putting the question: "Which became the best high jumper?" The incident is a coin with two sides; on one side there is justice and, on the other, grace. An obsession on the grace side is tantamount to masochism or spiritual self-flagellation, whereas an obsession towards justice narrows and hardens the outlook and eliminates a whole area of surprise kindness and unsuspected benefits without which life would be miserably barren.

But, it may be argued, this is not death and an innocent child's death at that! Are children all that innocent? The Grand Duchess of *The Just Assassins* evidently didn't think so. Speaking of her little niece at whom Yanek had refused to throw the bomb, she said: "My niece has an unpleasant nature. She refuses to carry her alms to the poor herself. She is frightened of being soiled by touching them. Isn't she unjust?" (CT, 373) Whereas her husband whom Yanek did kill was kind and loving towards the peasants, and concerned about Justice! When Camus wrote this play he was seeking to demonstrate that "justice is at one and the same time an idea and an aspiration of the soul. Let us seek it from its human side without transforming it into this terrible passion which has mutilated so many." (CE, 268) His objective, as already mentioned in the chapter on *Early Influences*, was to show that the end does not justify the means; that the means should justify themselves. He saw a truth; namely, that justice is not safe unless it is curbed by moderation, and moderation is an aspect of grace: it is the assumption that all the evidence is probably not known and thus precipitate and

radical action might produce something other than the desired effect. He saw that justice, uncurbed by moderation, became a monster which drove ruthlessly to murder whilst killing spiritually and psychologically and, perhaps, finally physically those who espoused her cause. Everyone in *The Just Assassins* is a loser and the most tragic loser of all is Yanek, who has to put to death successively his love for Dora, his religious or spiritual life, his sympathy for the Grand Duchess, and finally, having little else left, his own body too.

Seeing the necessity for moderation is the fruit of humility. It is a reticence to act, on the basis of a personal judgment, beyond the point where there is absolute certainty that sufficient facts are known wholly to justify that action and that it would be safe from unforeseen contrary side-effects. Total devotion to justice without the safeguarding effect of the moderation of grace quickly turns to something altogether negative; it becomes, not a seeking of justice, but rather a campaign against injustice and is bent on destroying rather than building. It is personified in Stepan of *The Just Assassins*, who seems to have passed from love of Justice to hatred for the unjust.

Now Camus saw all this in life but, when he turned to consider God and spiritual things, humility and moderation vanished. Dr. Jekyll turned into Mr. Hyde and anything beyond his own concept of Justice was simply not taken into account as he set himself to fight against the injustice in the order of the Universe. Thus it was that Dr. Rieux "believed himself to be on the road to the truth in fighting against the creation as he found it." (CT, 1320) We can understand also how he could feel that "since the order of the world is shaped by death, mightn't it be better for God if we refuse to believe in Him and struggle with all our might against death." (CP, 117) His resolution is final—"Until my dying day I shall refuse to love this creation in which children are tortured." (CT, 1395) This is a fixed and set spiritual position, based upon an assumed concept of the injustice of God and a closed door to any further consideration as to whether that concept was questionable as to its adequacy.

To return very briefly to the first chapter, it was demonstrated that *The Two Sides of the Coin*, Camus's first work, was a literary portrayal of the awakening to spiritual awareness. It was seen that this awareness is alive and functioning when a person is open to

see both sides. Thus the young man of the first story saw coincidentally in himself both hatred and compassion for the old lady; and the seeing was spiritual. Saint-Exupéry helped by defining the spirit as that other face which lies back of things and occupies itself, not with the things themselves directly, but with what links them together. If ever one side should so fill the horizon as to obscure and displace the other, then the spirit would pass from full and open vision to absolute blindness. There is a fine balance in the words of the prophet: "What doth the Lord require of thee, but to do justly and to love mercy and to walk humbly with thy God." (*Micah*, 6.8) If a man reverses it and begins to love justice, then justice will possess him wholly and begin to drive him, and it will not be long before he finds he has lost any consciousness of mercy or grace; it is but a short step thence to his denying their existence. But Dr. Rieux did not deny the existence of grace, he seems rather to recognize it and his lack of it when he says: "It's something I haven't got; that I know." Clamence of *The Fall,* in one of his moments of deadly earnestness, showed he had discerned a superhuman quality in Jesus Christ: "The unfortunate thing is that he left us alone to carry on . . . knowing in turn what he knew, but incapable of doing what he did and of dying as he died." (CT, 1532) Yet, almost in the same breath immediately prior to this he had said: "He was not superhuman, you can take my word for it. He cried aloud in his agony and that's why I love him, my friend who died without knowing." Superhuman and yet human; surely one who sees this much is not far from awakening to grace.

Index